# REFLECTIONS

## ON SCRIPTURE, DANDELIONS, AND SPARROWS

## WANDA THOMPSON

Energion Publications
Gonzalez, Florida
2018

Scripture quotations marked CEV are from the Contemporary English Version, Copyright © 1995 American Bible Society.

Scripture quotations marked NCV are from The Holy Bible, New Century Version, Copyright © 1987, 1988, 1991 by Word Publishing, Dallas, Texas 75039. Used by permission.

Scripture quotations marked NIV are from the HOLY BIBLE, NEW INTERNATIONAL VERSION®. Copyright © 1973, 1978, 1984 by International Bible Society. Used by permission of Zondervan Publishing House. All rights reserved.

Scripture quotations marked NKJV are from the New King James Version®. Copyright © 1982 by Thomas Nelson, Inc. Used by permission. All rights reserved.

Scripture quotations marked NRSV are from the New Revised Standard Version Bible. Copyright © 1989 by the Division of Christian Education of the National Council of the Churches of Christ in the U. S. A. Used by permission. All rights reserved.

Scripture quotations marked MSG are from THE MESSAGE®. Copyright © 1993, 1994, 1995, 1996, 2000, 2001, 2002. Used by permission of NavPress Publishing Group.

Scripture quotations marked TEV are from the Good News Translation in Today's English Version-Second Edition. Copyright © 1992 by American Bible Society. Used by Permission.

Scripture quotations marked HN were translated by Henry Neufeld. More complete translations can be found at jevlir.com.

Front Cover Photo: Wanda Thompson, *Olstinden*, near Reine, Lofoten Islands, Norway
Page iv Art: Wanda Thompson, ink and watercolor painting: *The Woodlot*, Eddleston, Scotland
Back Cover Art: Wanda Thompson, graphite drawing: *Beech Tree*, Eddleston, Scotland

Devotional Edition  ISBN: 978-1-63199-612-2
Library of Congress Control Number: 2018935548


Energion Publications
P. O. Box 841
Gonzalez, Florida 32560


energion.com
pubs@energion.com

For my Family

Alden,

Karin and Tom, Krista and Steve

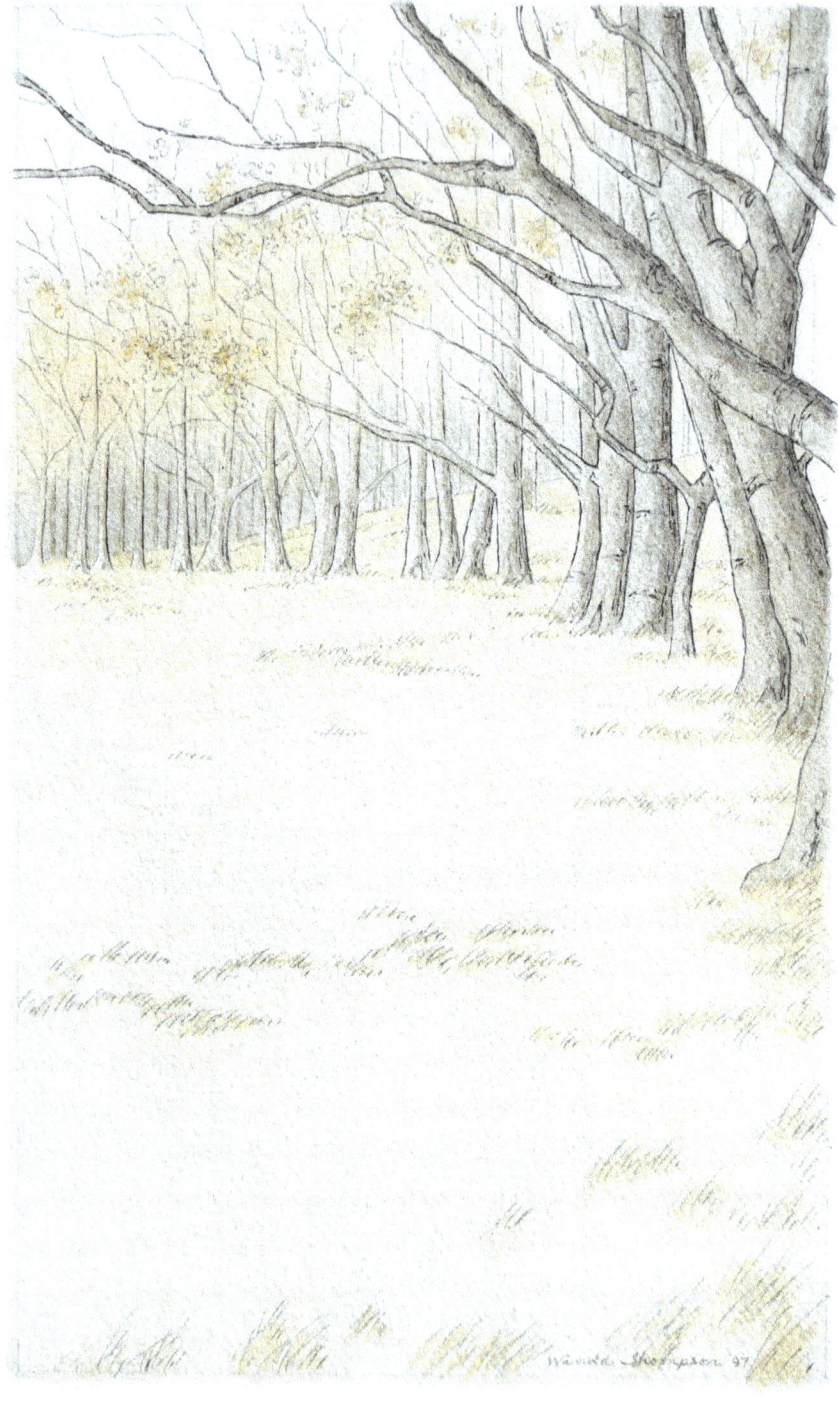

Wanda Thompson 97

# CONTENTS

# PREFACE

Almost every morning I walk past the small ponds, Eastloch and Westloch, and along Kirkhope Burn to Portmore Loch. As I walk I listen to the stream and robins and blackbirds and dandelions. Sometimes I watch raindrops falling or gently blowing grass or leaves flying in the wind. And I like to see what the clouds are up to.

Now and then I write down a few thoughts about these moments. But—

> How can I weave the call of chickadees into my words
> or the slow flowing song of the summer stream?
> How can I write the brightness of icy heron tracks on the winter pond?
> Or include the sound of high wind in the tops of the cottonwood trees?
> How can I add swallows zipping by
> or glorious clouds that drip lightly?
> So you can know?

The majority of these thoughts and observations are of what I see each day near my home, but some are of my visits to faraway places. I am not a writer and none of these reflections were intended for publication. But perhaps this book will encourage someone to write their own reflections on Scripture as a way of gaining fresh perspectives, and I hope it will inspire further appreciation and respect for nature.

"If you want to learn, then go and ask the wild animals and the birds, the flowers and the fish. Any of them can tell you what the Lord has done" Job 12:7–9 (CEV).

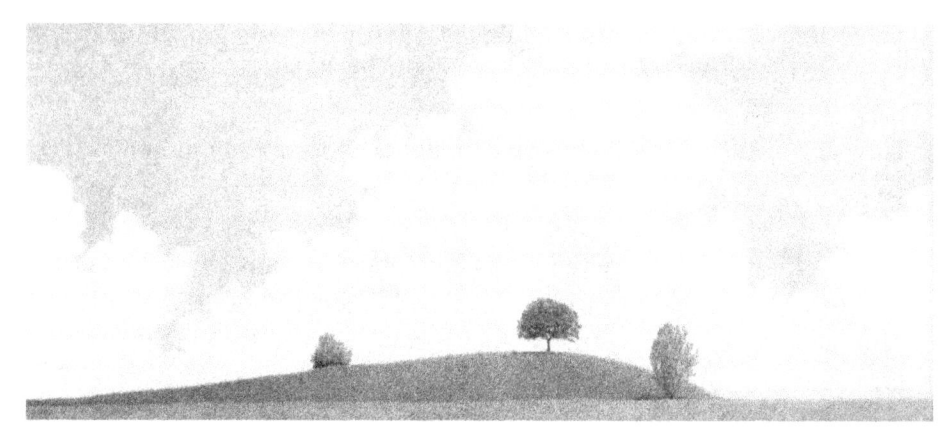

## PSALM 23:1–4 (NRSV/NCV/NKJV/ADAPTED)

"The Lord is my shepherd,
I shall not want."

"He lets me rest in green pastures"
where dandelions and bright grasses grow,
with tiny white flowers too
and maybe a cheerful weed here and there.

"He leads me beside still waters"
where only the wind ripples the surface
and perhaps a swan swims by.

"He restores my soul"
by showing me raindrops
holding on to a blackberry briar,
often with a sparrow singing nearby.

"He leads me in paths of righteousness"
that go up past the waterfall to Coire Lagan
or through the puddles along the River Tweed
on a rainy day.

"Even if I walk through the valley
of the shadow of death,
I will not fear evil
because he is with me.
His rod and staff comfort me"
by reminding me
that the Lord is my shepherd.

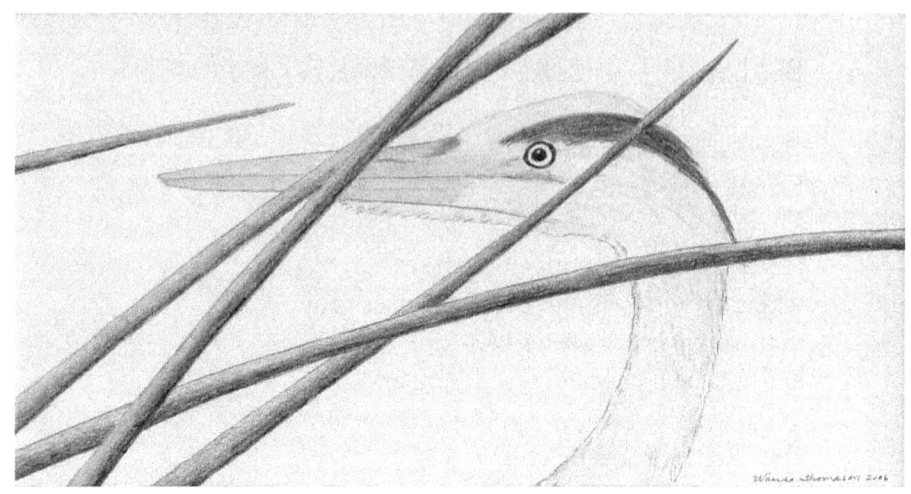

Psalm 118:24 (NIV)

"This is the day the Lord has made;
let us rejoice and be glad in it."

Yes. I'm rejoicing
and I'm glad this day.
I'm glad for baby geese on the pond
and the great heron.
I'm glad for wild roses blooming by the stream
and the sound of the stream too.
I rejoice in clouds of glory
and flocks of starlings in the sky.
I'm glad when the air is silent
and I can hear quail talking in the bushes.
Yes. I rejoice.
I'm glad this day.

Isaiah 55:12 (NIV)

"You will go out in joy and be led forth in peace"
      through heather hills or buttercup fields;
"the mountains and hills will burst into song before you"
      as the grand choir of the Dolomites fills the air,
"and all the trees of the field will clap their hands"—
      which is what they do along the drive to Drummond Castle!

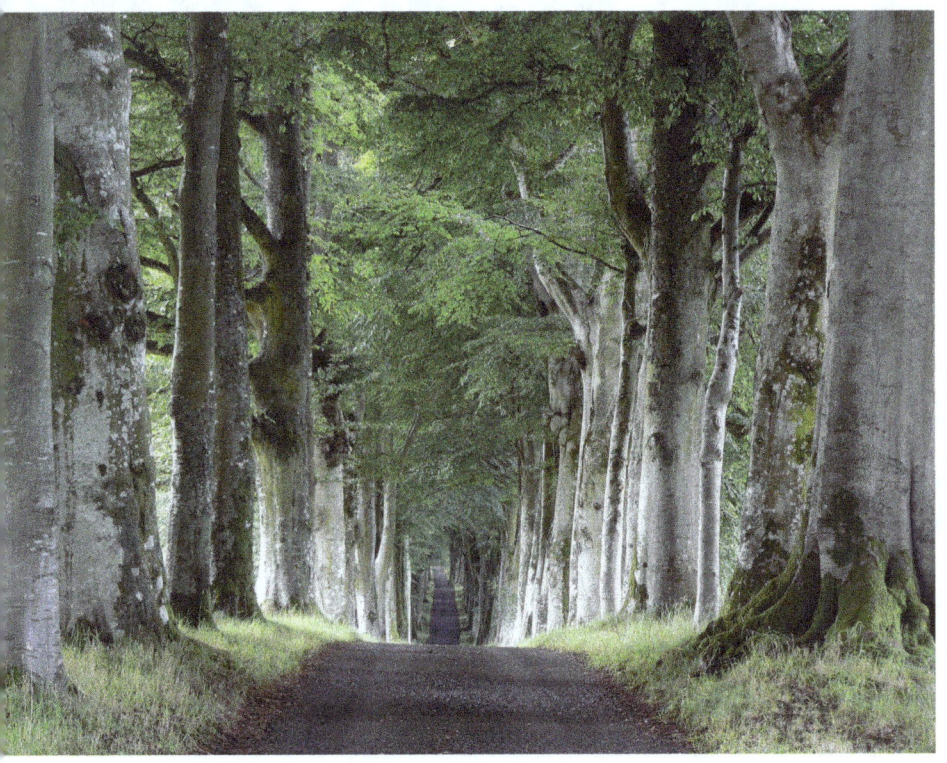

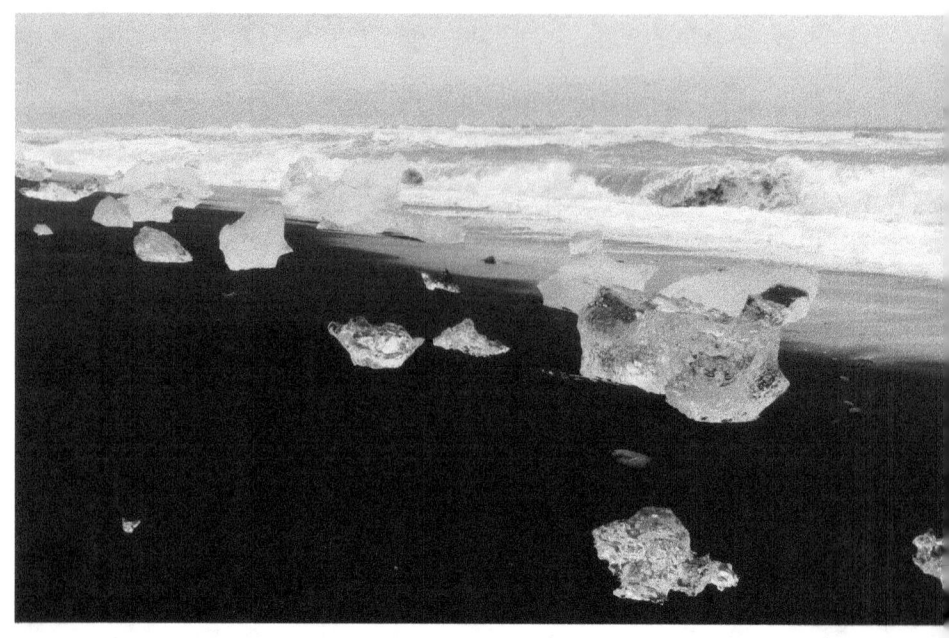

## LUKE 1:78 (CEV)

"God's love and kindness will shine upon us
like the sun that rises in the sky."

Like buttercups that shine in the grass
or clouds that glow from the heavens.

Like moon reflections that glimmer
on the crests of sea waves.

Like ice sculptures that glisten
along the beach at Jökulsárlón.

## PSALM 37:7 (NRSV)

"Be still before the Lord,
and wait patiently for him."

I'll compose my life from stillness.
That's not silence, just quietness.
I'll listen to a grasshopper snapping in dry weeds
and to the soft breeze in the autumn leaves.
I'll take time to hear the stream flowing
and chickadees flitting in the brush.
I'll listen until the goldfinch finishes its song.
Maybe I can hear bees humming
and the whir of flying quail
or even a cricket purring in the hot grass
if I stop and listen.

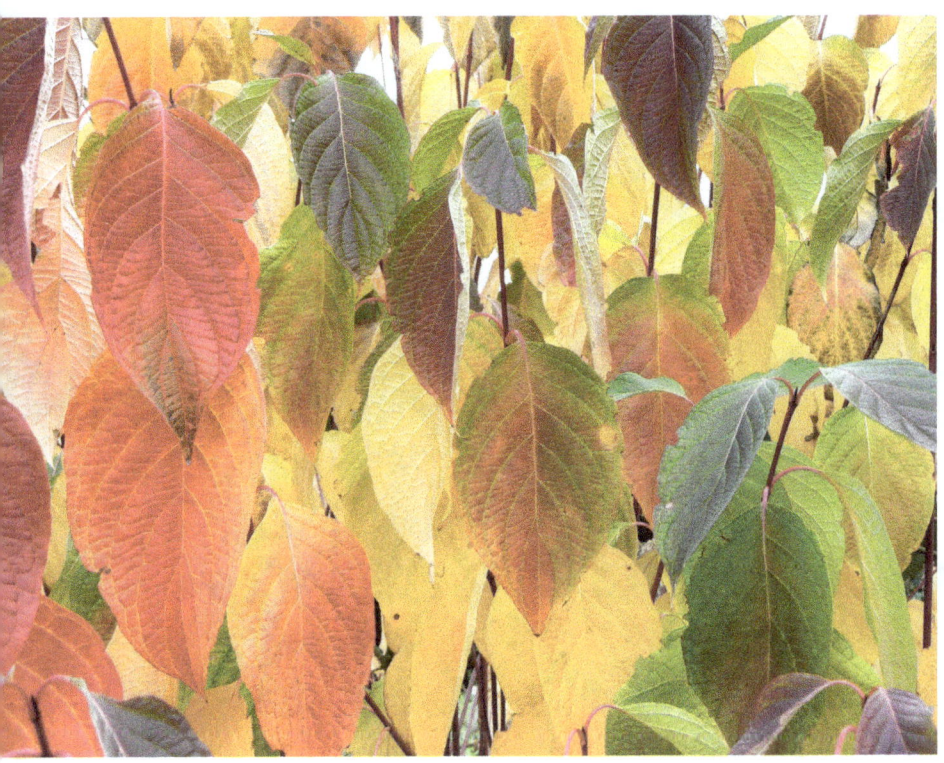

## PSALM 57:5 (NRSV)

"Be exalted, O God, above the heavens.
Let your glory be over all the earth."

Let whooper swans float on pink evening reflections.
Let horses play among buttercups
and snow mountains overlook green fields.
Let clear water fall with music over lava rocks.
Let lupines cover the land with a purple glow
and arctic terns fill the sky with gladness.
Let blue glacier ice brighten dark sand.

Yes, "Let your glory be over all the earth."

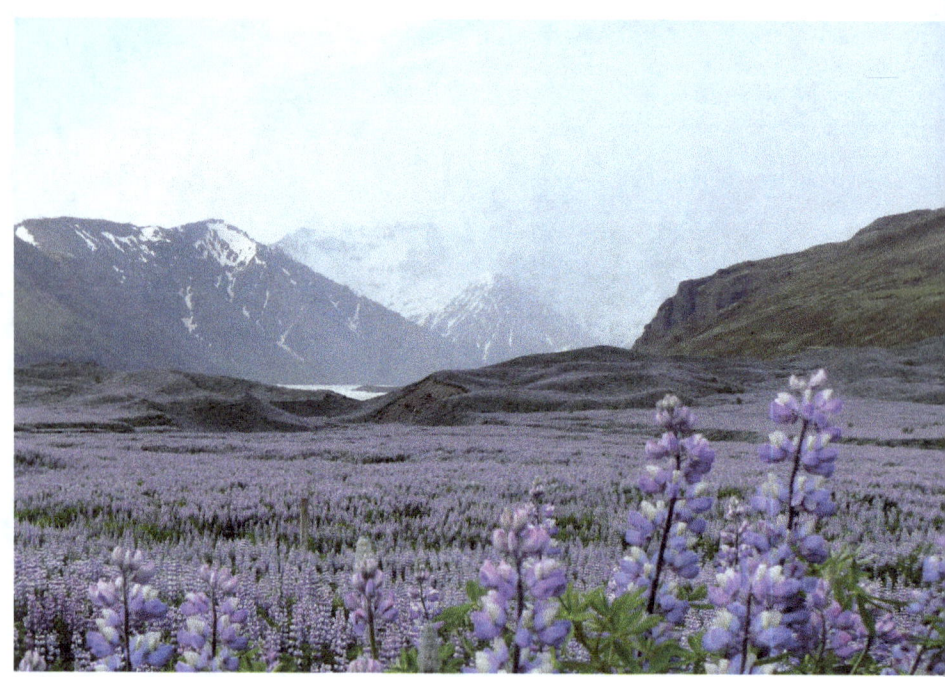

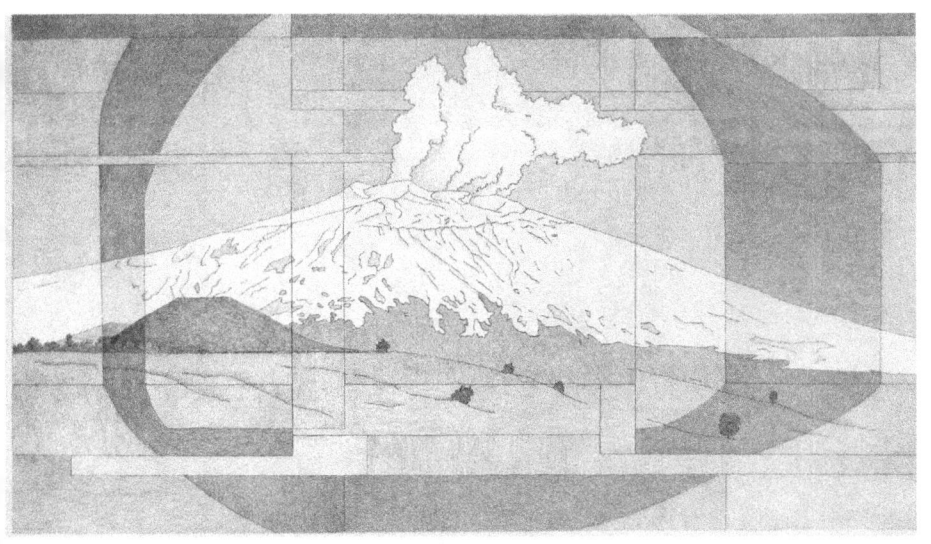

## ROMANS 1:20 (NRSV)

"Ever since the creation of the world
his eternal power and divine nature,
invisible though they are,
have been understood and seen
through the things he has made."

Mount Etna's spectacular eruptions,
the extreme force of Trümmelbachfälle,
and the wild wind and waves of Dyrhólaey
help us understand his eternal power.
His divine nature is seen in morning frost,
in the gentle eyes of a deer,
and in pink and white daisies along my path.

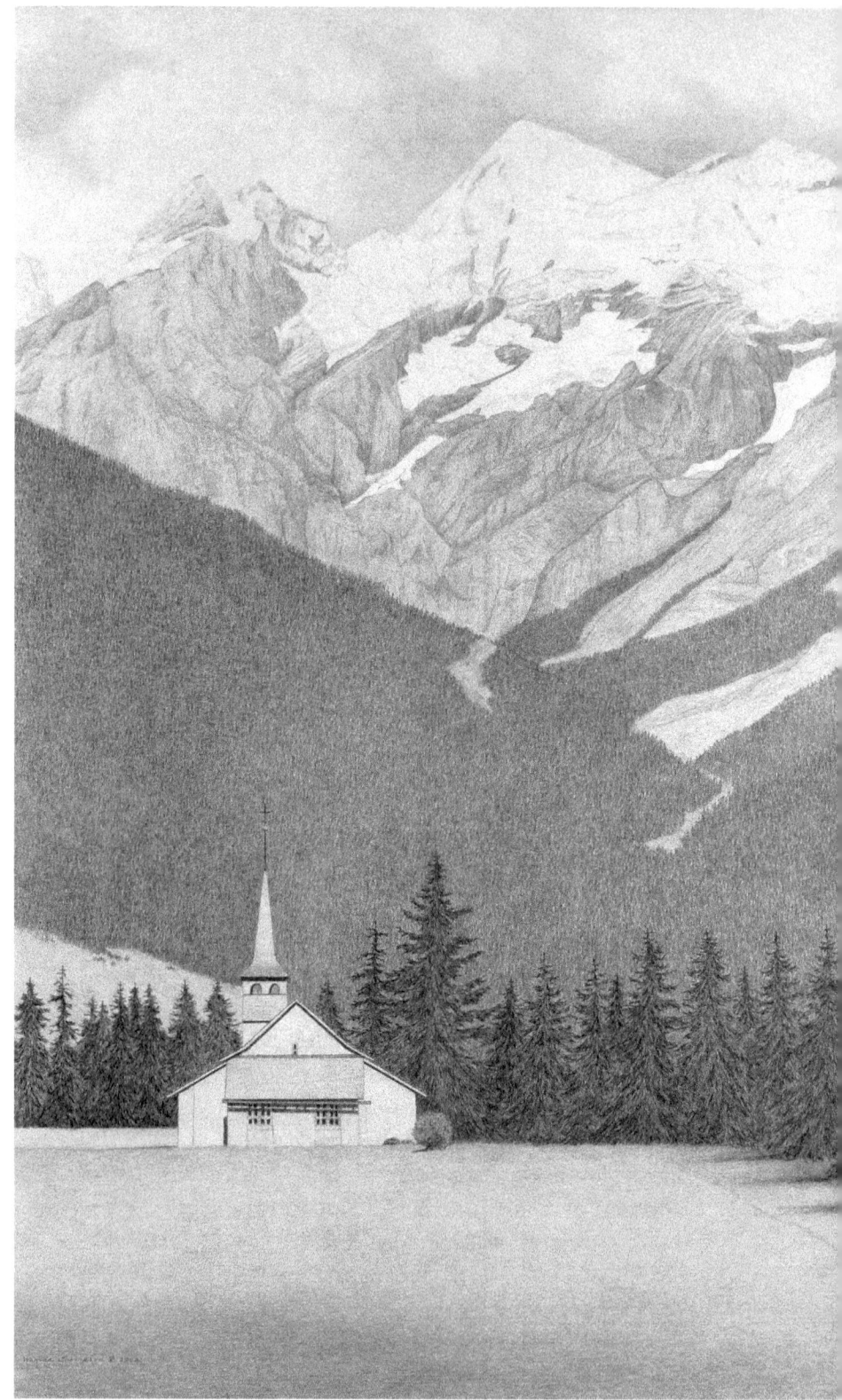

ISAIAH 49:13 (NIV)

"Shout for joy, O heavens!"
Stars and misty clouds,
rainbows and sunsets, shout for joy!

"Rejoice, O earth!"
Hills and valleys, rejoice
along with lakes and trees!

"Burst into song, O mountains!"
Alps and Dolomites,
Eiger and Jungfrau,
break out with song day and night!

"For the Lord comforts his people
and will have compassion on his afflicted ones."
That's all of us, everywhere,
in Finland, Mexico, or New Zealand.

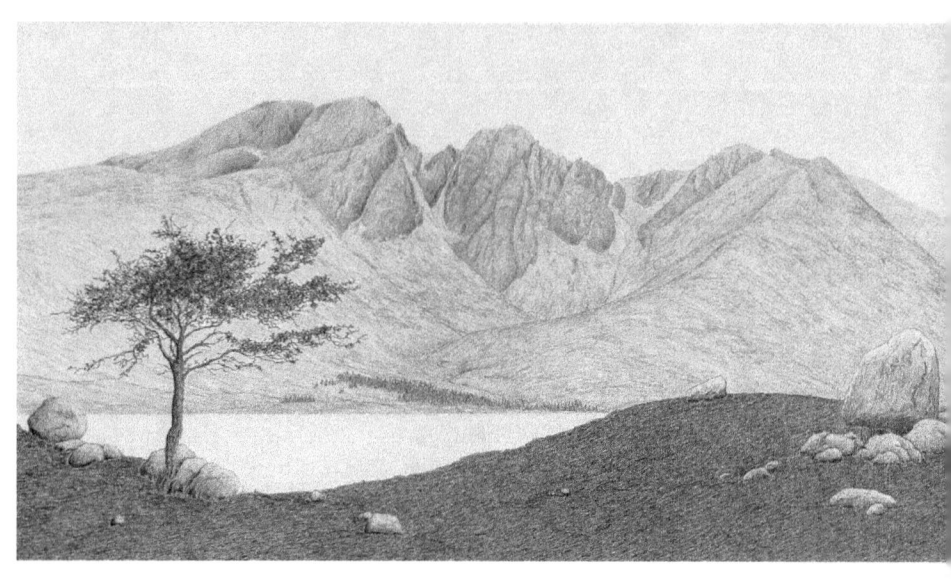

## JOHN 1:16 (NIV)

"From the fullness of his grace
we have all received
one blessing after another."

One sparrow after another
sings in the morning stillness;
one bright leaf after another
glows in the sunlight.

One misty cloud, and another,
sprinkles a few drops of rain;
one dandelion, and another,
shines yellow in the grass.

One morning glory after another
gaily blossoms along my path;
one friend after another
cheers my life with love.

LUKE 12:7 (NIV)

"Don't be afraid; You are worth more than many sparrows."

I think even one sparrow is worth quite a lot.
It sings joyfully and cheers my day with music.
Even if it repeats its song over and over
it is bright and beautiful every time.
It is a little friend
helping me along my path
to wherever I'm going.

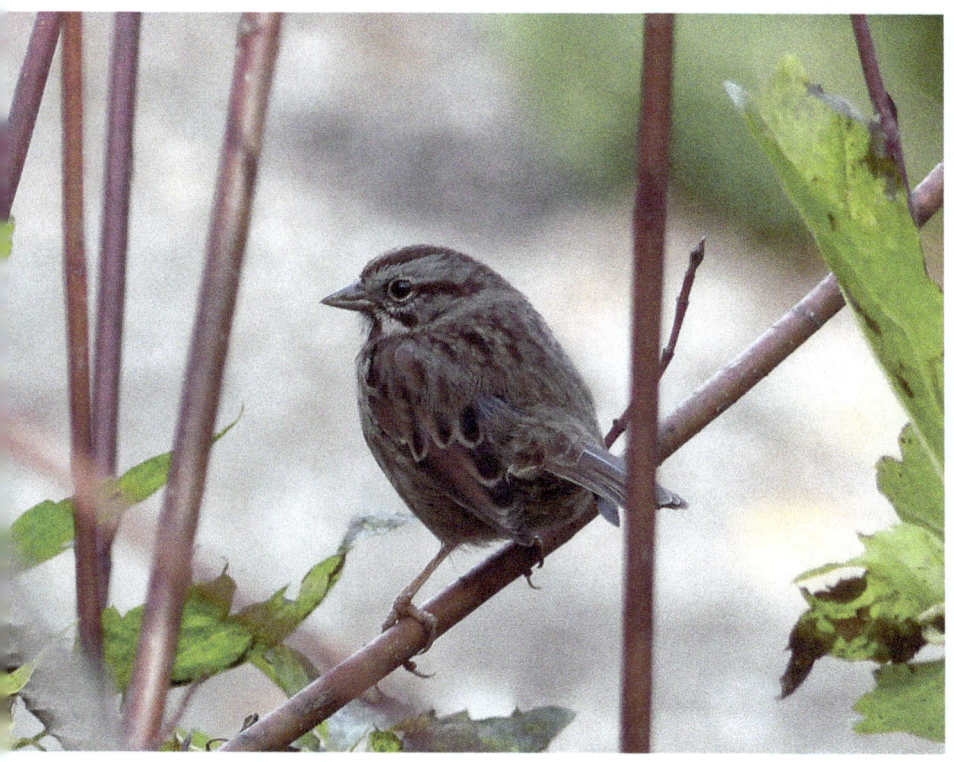

PSALM 9:1, 2 (NIV)

"I will praise you, O Lord, with all my heart,"
    a robin shouted from a branch above.
"I will tell of all your wonders,"
    blackbirds sang around the pond.
"I will be glad and rejoice in you,"
    geese called from the clouds.
"I will sing praise to your name, O Most High,"
    juncos answered from the bushes.

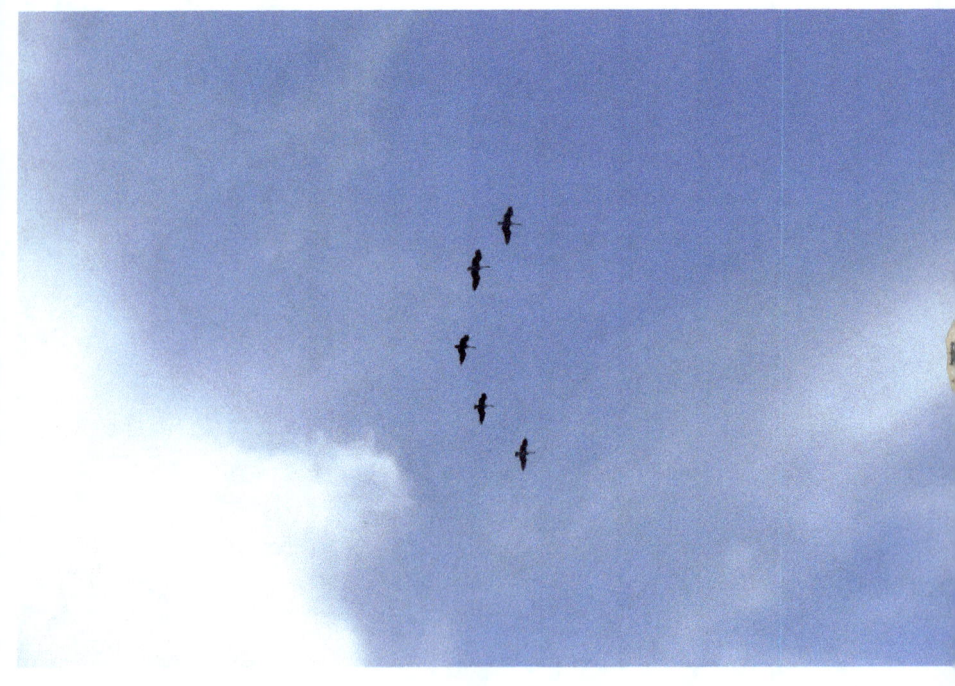

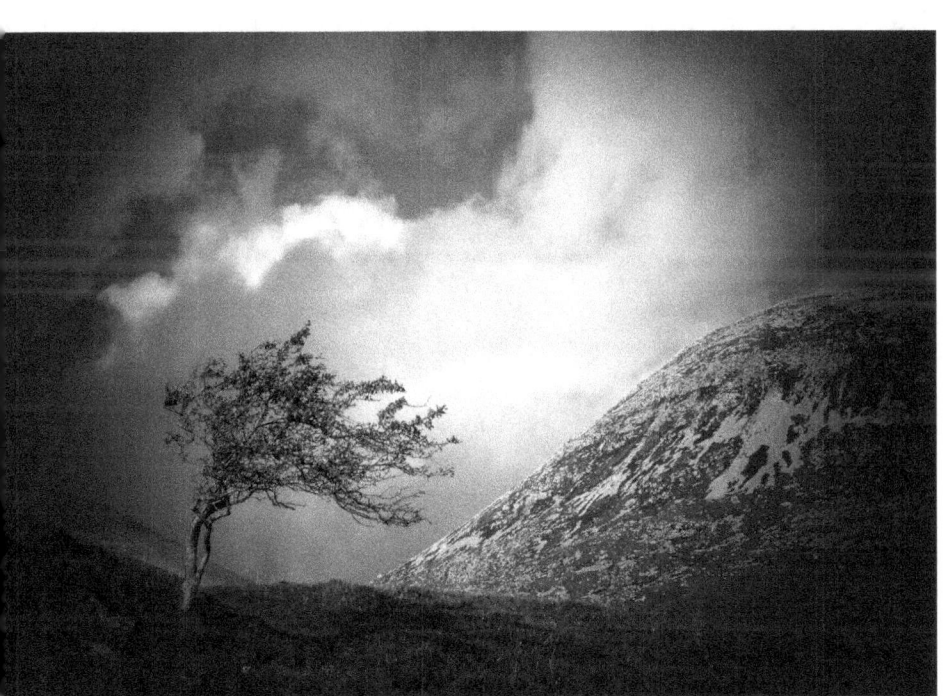

For God so loved the world
hat he gave his one and only Son,
hat whoever believes in him
hall not perish but have eternal life.
'or God did not send his Son
nto the world to condemn the world,
ut to save the world through him."

And that's not all he gave us!

He gave us fragrant wild roses,
playful squirrels,
and snowdrops in frosty grass.
He gave us smiling poppies,
flying geese,
and sparkling rivers.

High misty mountains are his gifts,
as well as chatting magpies
and owls calling in the dark.
He gave us humming bees,
blossoming weeds,
and fluffy clouds.

He gave us happiness,
love, and hope.

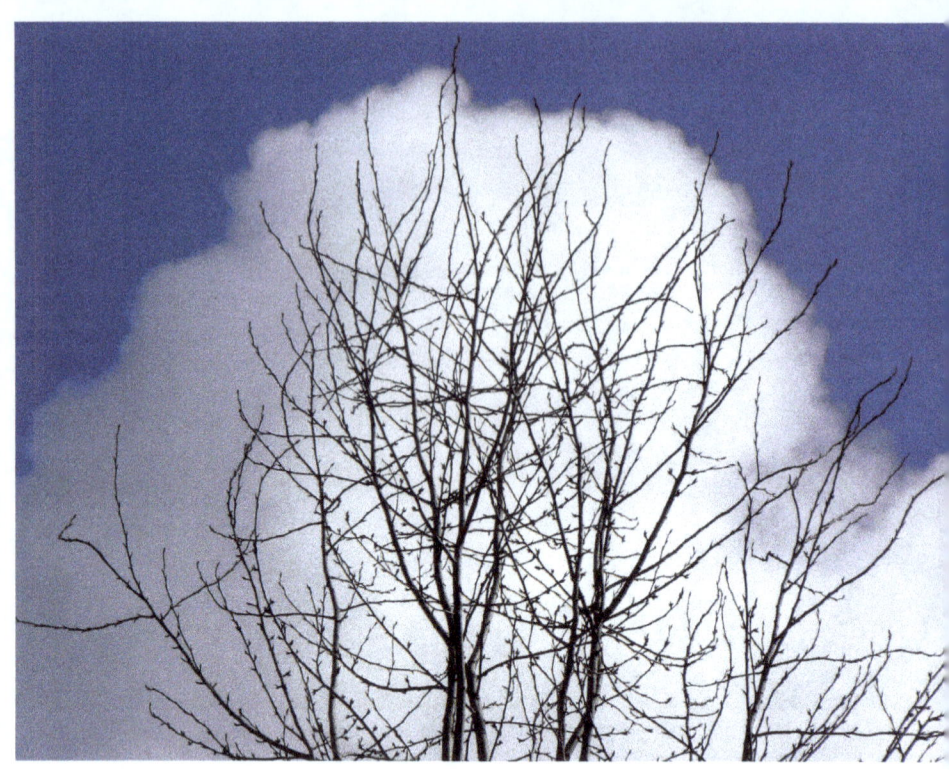

## PSALM 57:5 (HN)

"Your greatness, O God, is shown in the sky,
and your glory over all the earth."

A great golden cloud
rises above the trees.
As it reaches higher
it grows brighter.
It turns pink
in the setting sun.
Soon the cloud cools
and fades into gray.
A half-moon and Venus
watch from above.
Then lightning flashes
from the great cloud
and night covers us.

## JOHN 3:8 (NRSV)

"The wind blows where it chooses,
and you hear the sound of it,
but you do not know
where it comes from
or where it goes."

The wind
goes where it blows
among the robin trees
through sparrow briars
past the mallard pond
over blackbird cattails
across the killdeer field
up Hawk Hill—
then where does it go?

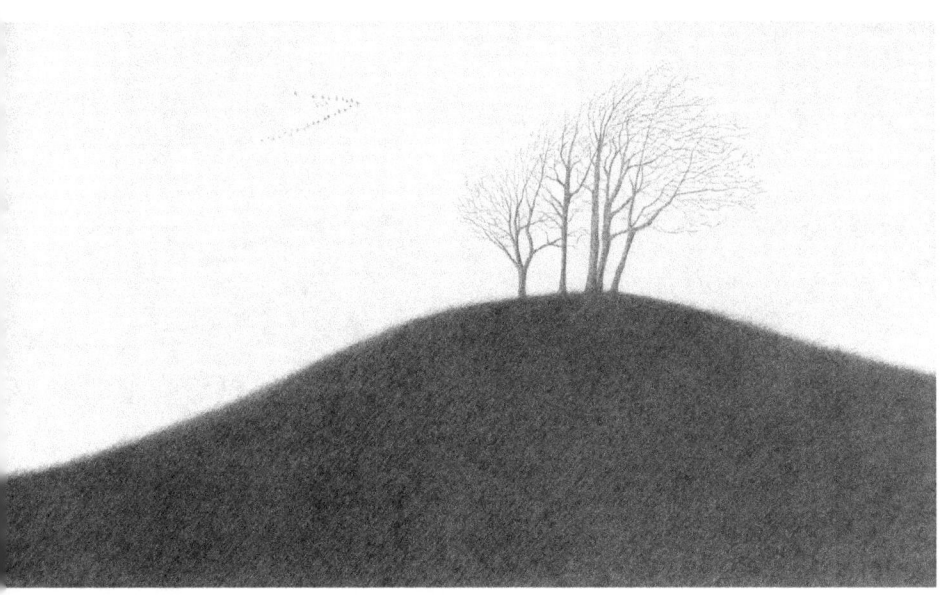

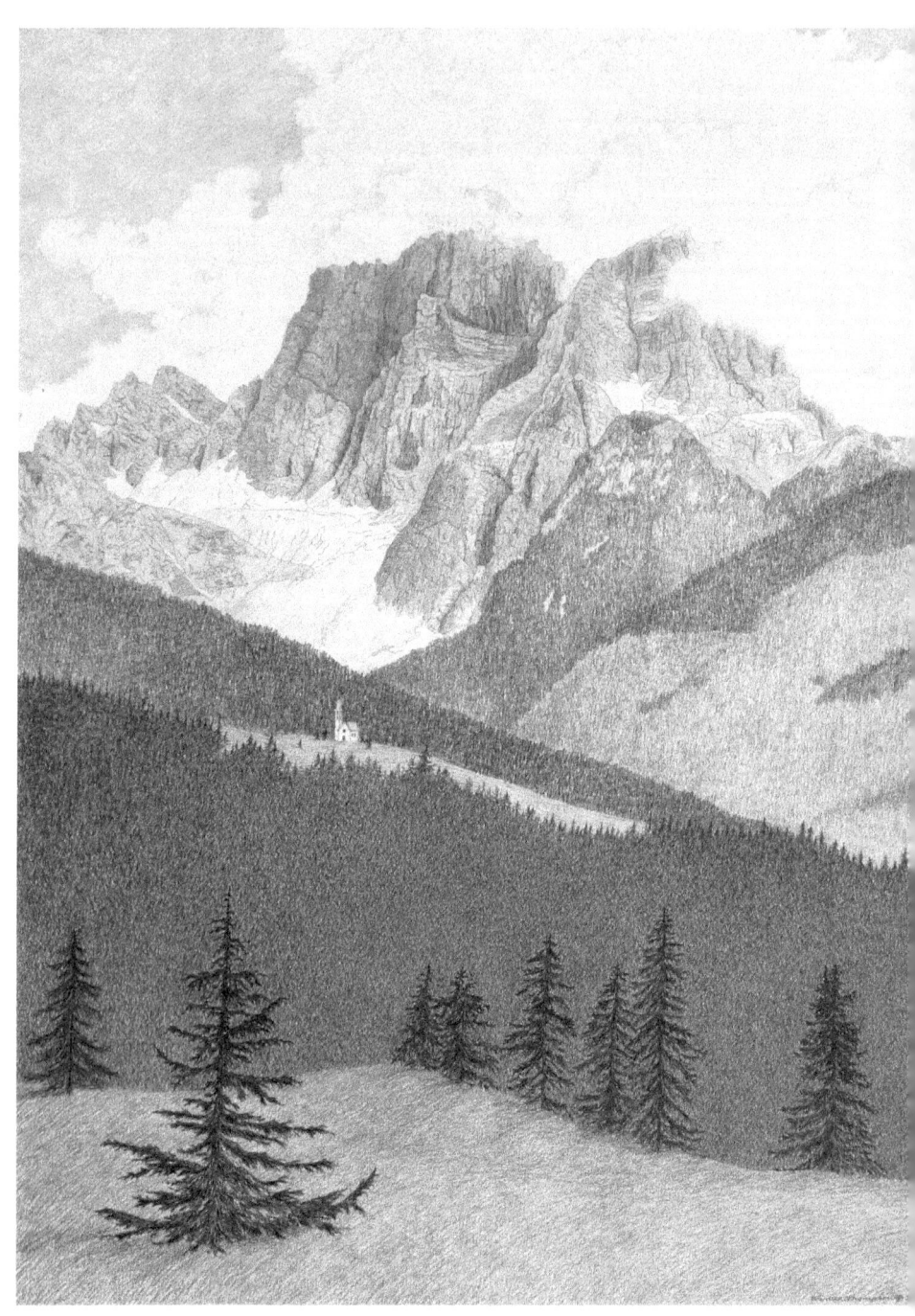

PSALM 96:1, 11–13 (NRSV)

"Oh sing to the Lord a new song;
sing to the Lord, all the earth. . . .
Let the heavens be glad,
and let the earth rejoice;
let the sea roar,
and all that fills it;
let the field exult,
and everything in it.
Then shall the trees of the forest
sing for joy before the Lord."

What music would the meadow sing
if each daisy sang a note?
Gounod's "Sanctus"?
What music would the forest sing
if each tree sang a note?
Mozart's "Laudate Dominum"?
What music would the mountain sing
if each rock and pebble sang a note?
Handel's "Hallelujah Chorus"?
What music would the sky sing
if each cloud sang a note?
Mendelssohn's *Elijah*?

PSALM 145:5 (NIV)

"I will meditate on your wonderful works."

I just took time
to think my thoughts
feel the breeze
listen to the stream run
hear the sparrow song
watch the shadows move
feed the ducklings

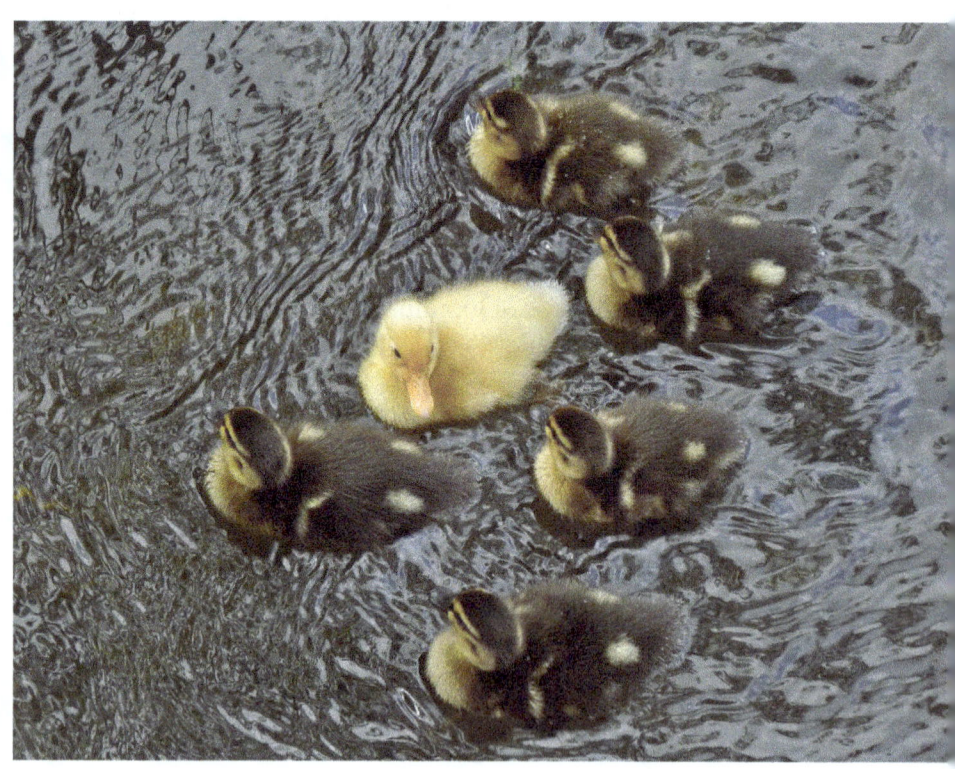

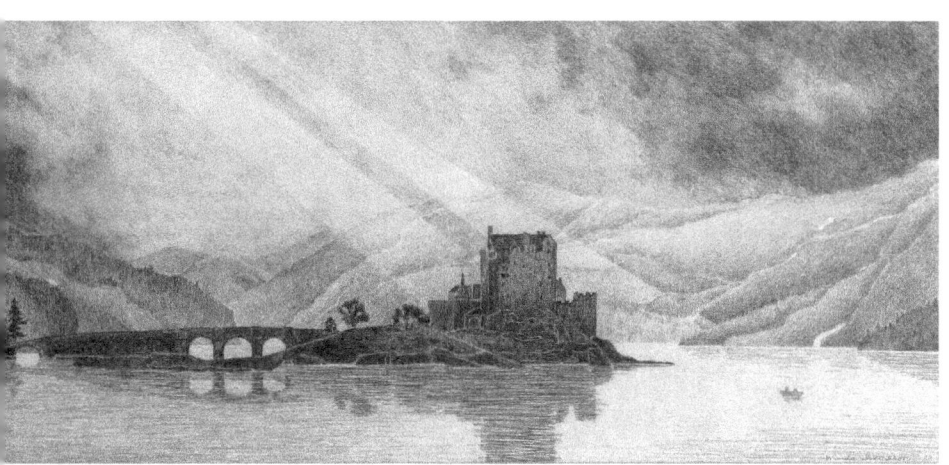

LUKE 5:26 (NIV)

"Everyone was amazed and gave praise to God.
They were filled with awe and said,
'We have seen remarkable things today.'"

Well, I didn't exactly see a miracle today
but I am amazed and praise God
for the remarkable things I've seen.
Clouds, for instance.
Over the dark mountains
they looked like higher mountains
with glaciers and deep snow.
Then I saw light streaming from the clouds
making the hills glow.
Later I saw two wild geese calling across the sky
until they disappeared beyond the top of the hill.
I was filled with awe and said,
"Yes, I have seen remarkable things today."

21

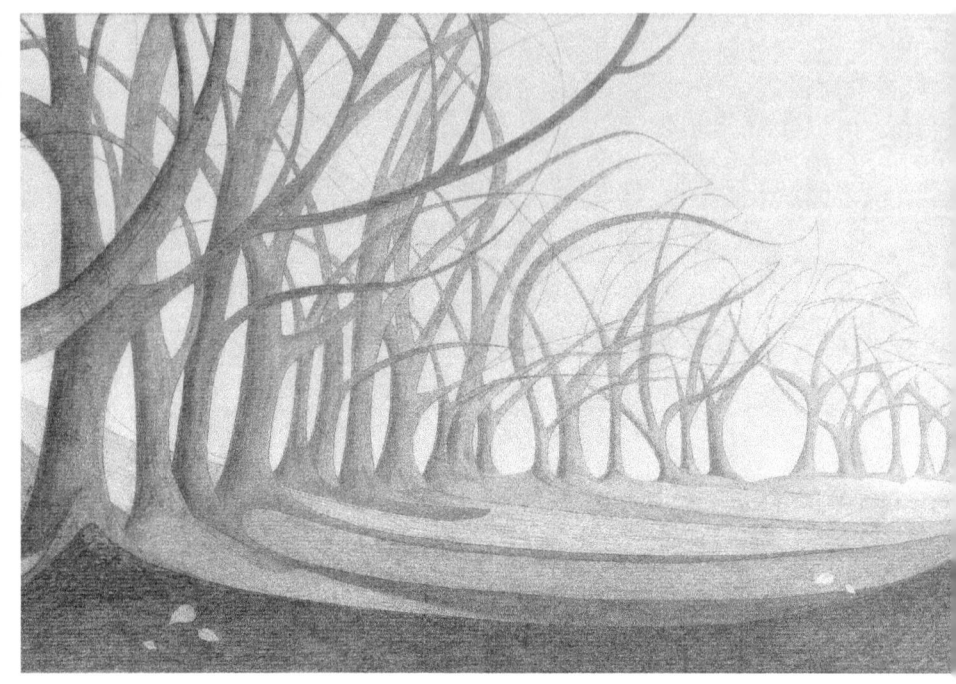

## MATTHEW 17:5 (NIV)

"This is my Son, whom I love;
with him I am well pleased.
Listen to him!"

I can't hear his voice speaking words aloud to me
but I am listening.

What is he saying to me in the curlew's call?
What is he saying to me in the sound of the wandering stream?
Is he saying something to me in the chattering of squirrels?
Or in wind rushing through the beech trees?

## SONG OF SONGS 2:10–14 (MSG)

"Spring flowers are in blossom all over.
The whole world's a choir—and singing!
Spring warblers are filling the forest
with sweet arpeggios.
Lilacs are exuberantly purple and perfumed,
and cherry trees fragrant with blossoms."

Do you like to rest in violets
with purple fragrance surrounding you?
Do you like to run in grass
with bluebells chiming in the wind?
Do you like to follow geese
calling from the clouds
or walk with robins,
taking moments to listen now and then?
Do you like to watch busy sandpipers
searching around the pond
or listen to humming blossoms
on springtime apple trees?

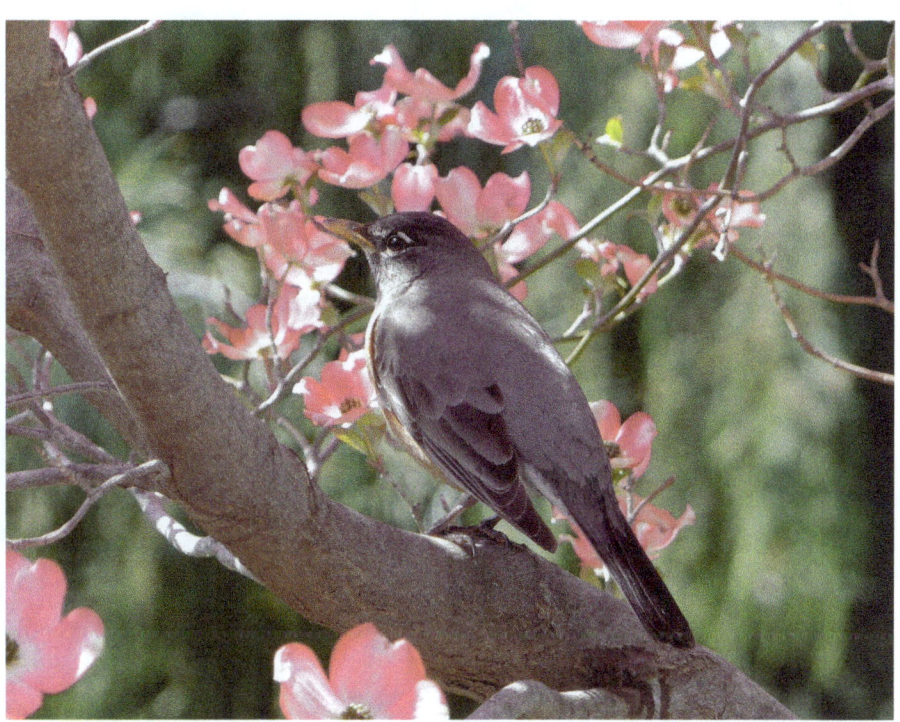

PSALM 100:1, 2 (TEV)

"Sing to the Lord, all the world!
Worship the Lord with joy;
come before him with happy songs!"

They must be happy,
those dandelions.
They are always smiling
and they are quite friendly too.

Sometimes they droop a little
when they get old
but then they fluff out
and glow white in the sun.

If it rains and they get wet
they don't smile so much
but I think they are still happy
because they keep on singing.

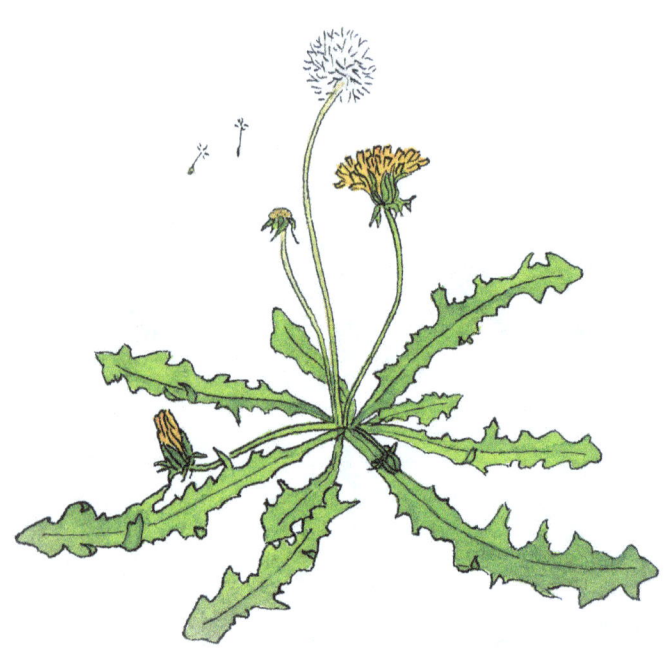

24

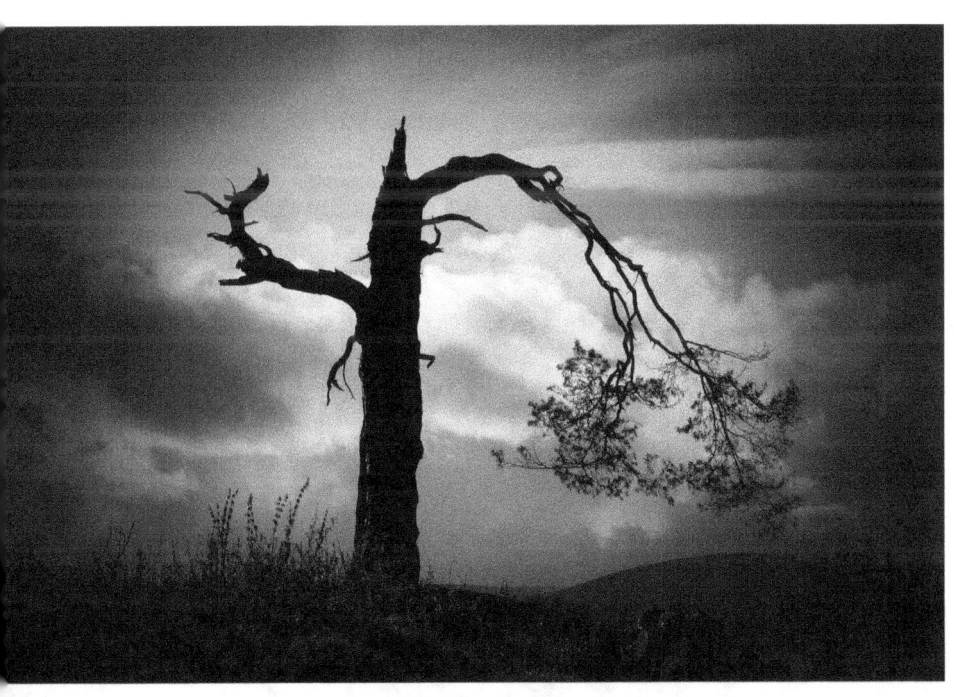

PSALM 34:3 (TEV)

"Proclaim with me the Lord's greatness;
let us praise his name together!"

The voice of wind praises the Lord
as it sings among the trees.
The voice of thunder proclaims his greatness
as it crashes through dark clouds.
The river's voice praises his name
as it hurries over mossy stones
and little wren voices singing without words
praise God.
Yes, "let us praise his name together!"

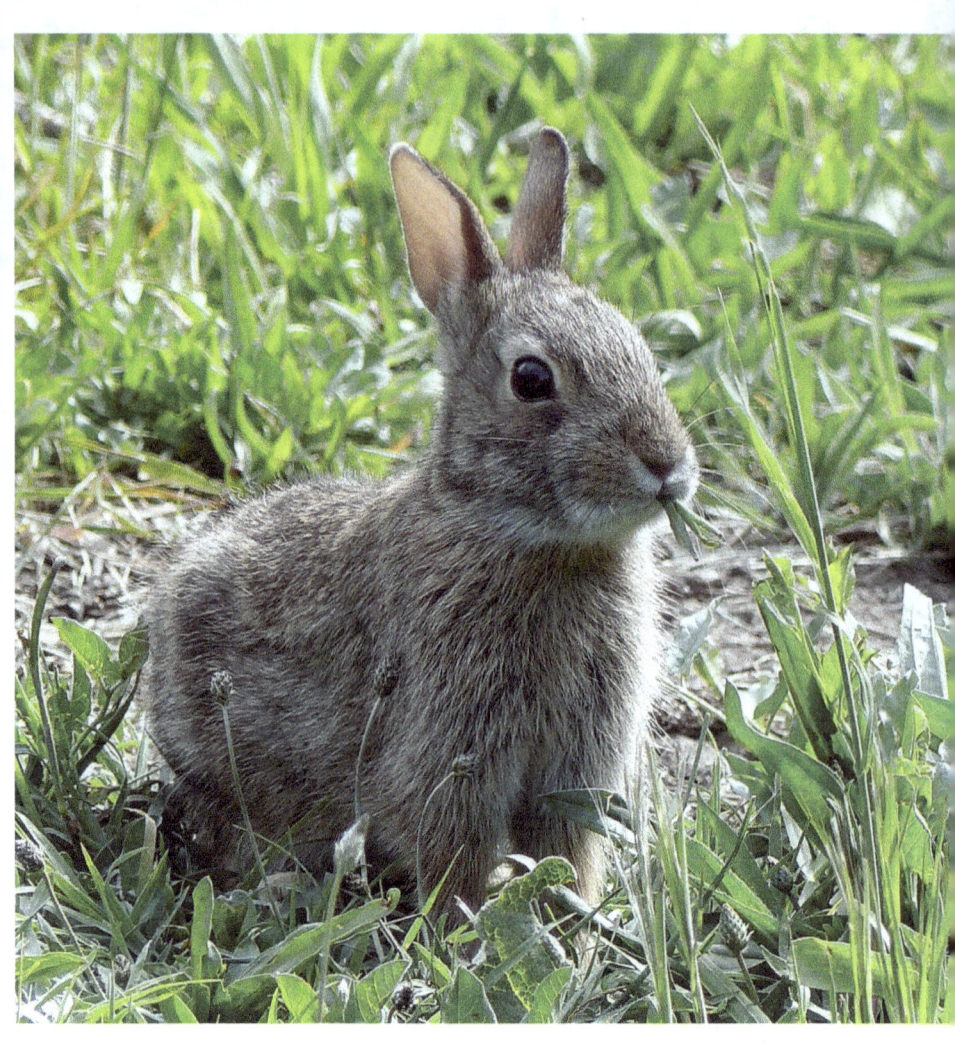

## PSALM 50:10, 11 (HN)

"Each animal living in the forest is mine,
  flocks and herds on unnumbered hills.
I know every bird in the wild;
  even crickets are in my care."

If you walk softly
and don't have a dog
you might be able to come quite close
to the little rabbit eating grass
beside the blackberry briars.

If you listen carefully
and aren't in a great hurry
you might be able to hear
quail softly clucking
far back in the bushes.

If you watch attentively
and take your time
you might be able to glimpse
a ruby-crowned kinglet flitting
among the willow leaves.

If you stand quietly
and wait a few minutes
you might be able to see
a muskrat swimming
across the sunlit pond.

"O come, let us sing to the Lord. . . .
Let us make a joyful noise to him
with songs of praise!"

## THE GREAT CHORAL SYMPHONY

The sparrow solo was magnificent!
The rest of the choir outstanding too.
I especially enjoyed the robin chorus
together with the doves and flickers,
chickadees, juncos, blackbirds,
and downy woodpecker percussion.
Even the magpies did their part well.
Perhaps the crows were a bit off
but it was all glorious just the same.
By the way, if you missed today's concert
a repeat performance is scheduled for tomorrow.

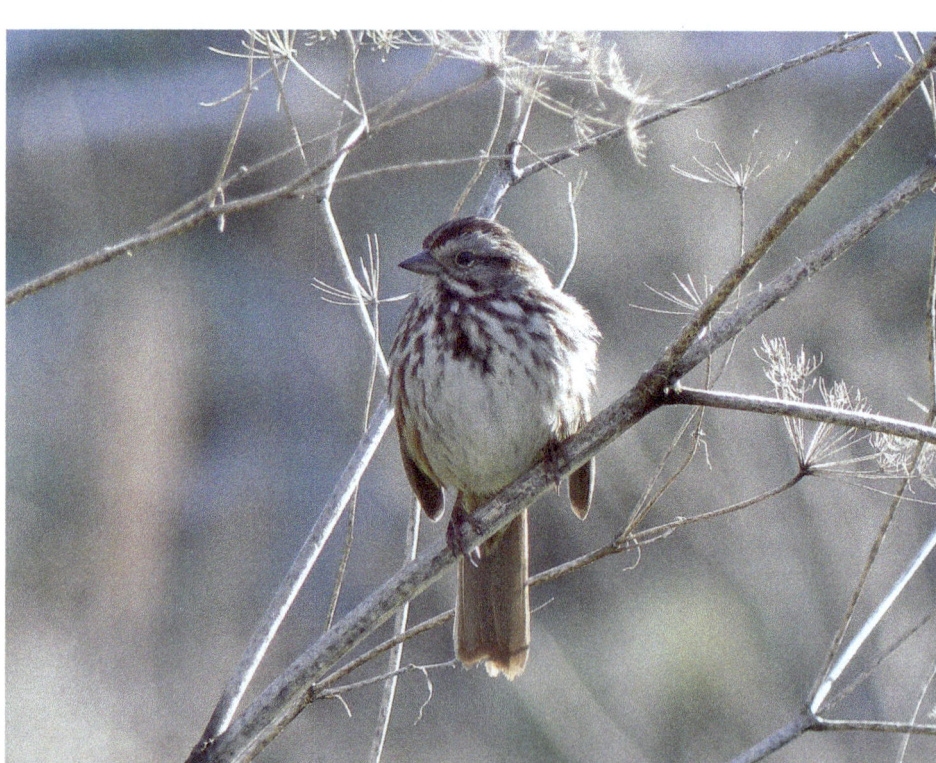

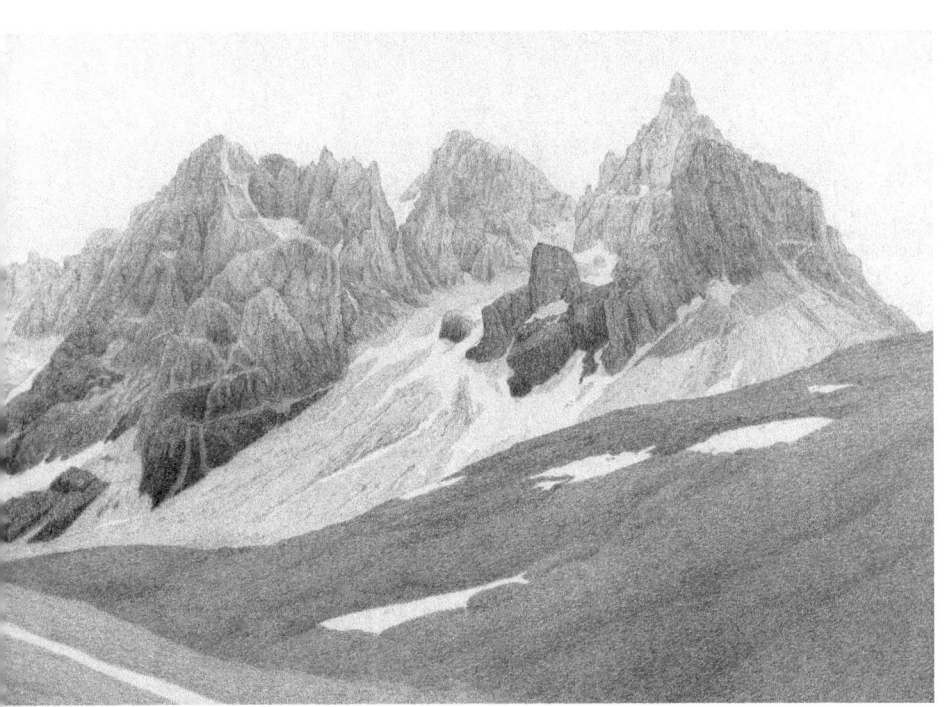

## PSALM 72:3 (NKJV)

"The mountains will bring peace to the people."

High on the mountaintops
where snow stays
alpine choughs soar in the clouds
while tiny purple gentians
huddle in the short grass.
A stony path wanders up
along fast streams and waterfalls
to where snow stays.
A few small trees reach upward,
wanting to be there,
while I stand gazing higher,
longing to be up where snow stays.

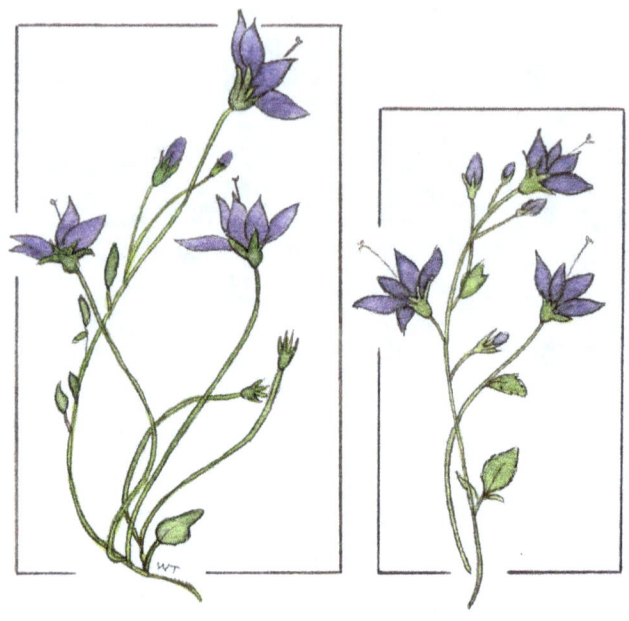

I Chronicles 16:10 (NRSV)

"Let the hearts of those who seek the Lord rejoice."

Dandelions are smiling everywhere
among the sparkling drops
from last night's rain.
These other purple flowers
are probably smiling too
but they don't have big faces
like dandelions so it is harder to tell.
Their faces are small and hidden down inside.
But whatever kind of face you have,
your smile can brighten someone's day.

## PSALM 103:5 (NIV)

"He satisfies my desires
with good things."

I like being in a crowd—
a crowd of trees
with a crowd of birds,
a crowd of grass
with a crowd of wildflowers,
a crowd of mountains
with a crowd of clouds on top.

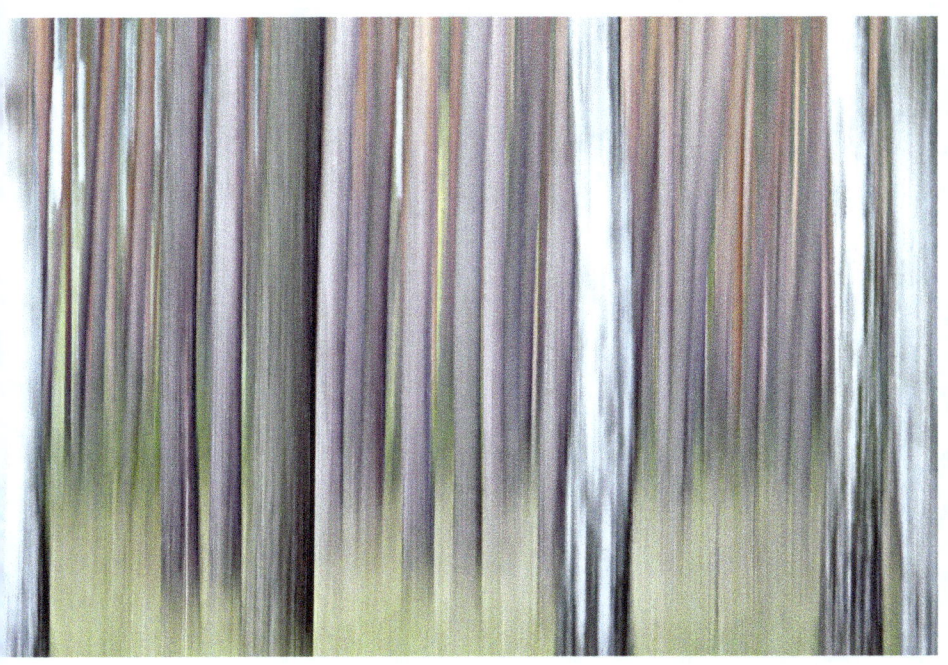

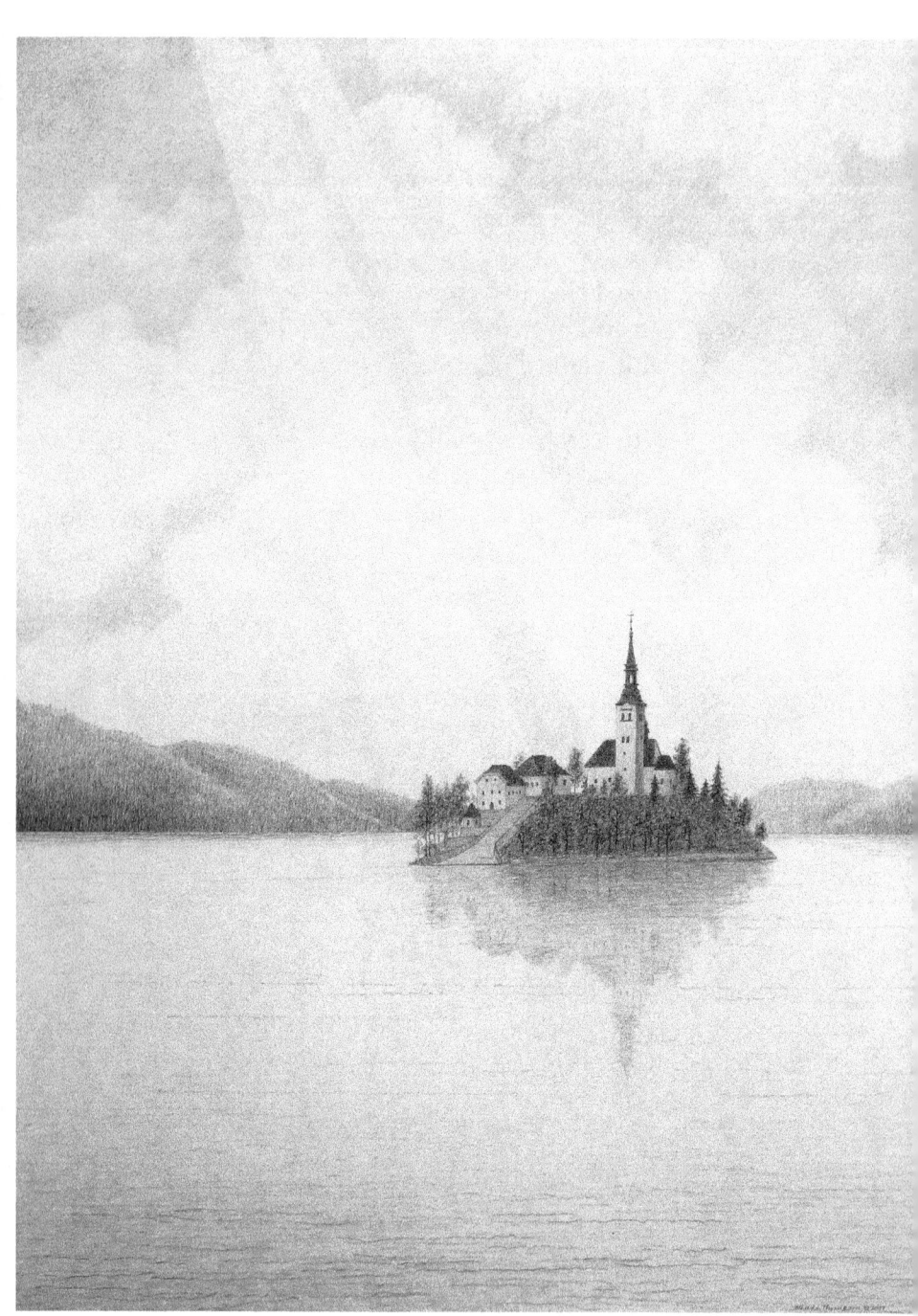

## II Corinthians 4:6 (NIV)

"For God, who said, 'Let light shine out of darkness,'
made his light shine in our hearts to give us the light
of the knowledge of the glory of God in the face of Christ."

The morning sky is alive with clouds dancing
over the mountaintops where the sun comes up.
They look excited about the new day
and become brighter each moment
as the sun rises behind them.
I think God's smile is coming down through the clouds
on the bright rays of light that stream across my day.

## PSALM 104:24 (NIV)

"How many are your works, O Lord!
In wisdom you made them all;
the earth is full of your creatures."

I'd rather walk with a robin.
Although it hurries along just ahead
it then waits for me to catch up
before hurrying ahead again.
At the end of our walk
as it flies away without me,
I reluctantly have to admit
I can't fly.

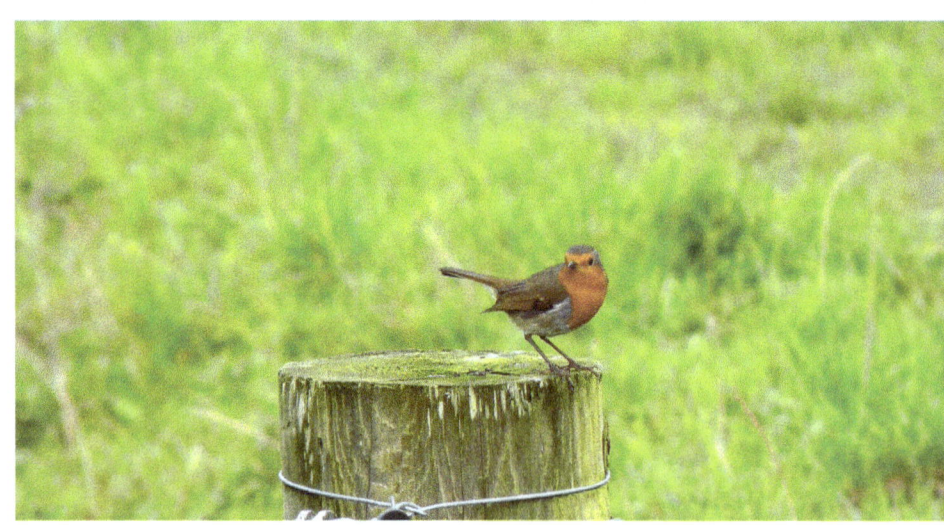

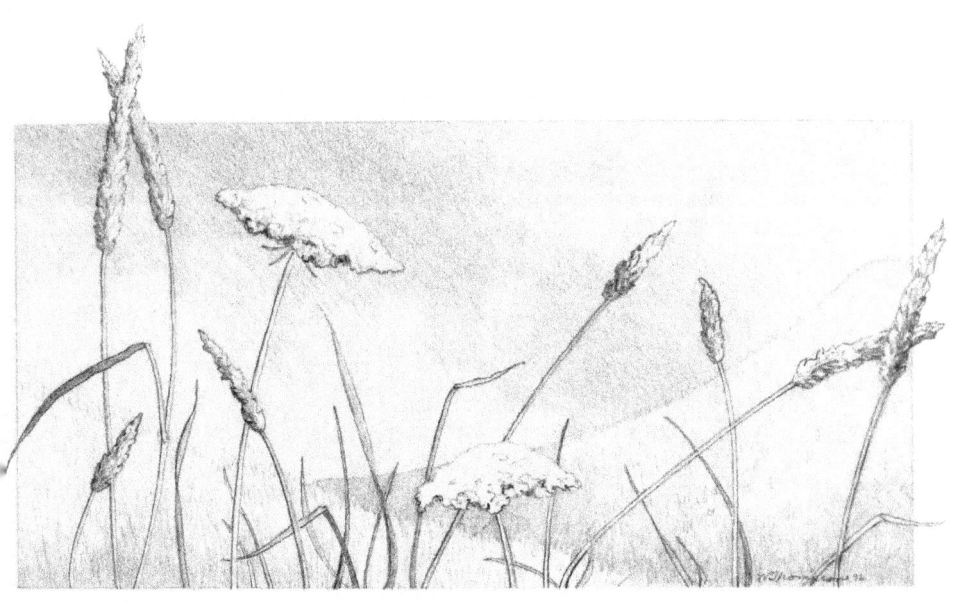

PSALM 24:1 (NRSV)

"The earth is the Lord's
and all that is in it."

I like weeds on a hillside.
They are such a happy mixture
of blossoms and colors,
grasses and shadows,
insects and leaves,
sunshine and shapes.

## PSALM 98:4, 7, 8 (NIV)

"Shout for joy to the Lord, all the earth,
burst into jubilant song with music. . . .
Let the sea resound, and everything in it,
the world, and all who live in it.
Let the rivers clap their hands,
let the mountains sing together for joy."

Soaring gulls and roaring wind
shout for joy to the Lord.
Pouring rain and sea waves
burst into jubilant song.
The little river at Elgol claps its hands
as it joins the sea music
and the misty Cuillin mountains
sing together for joy!

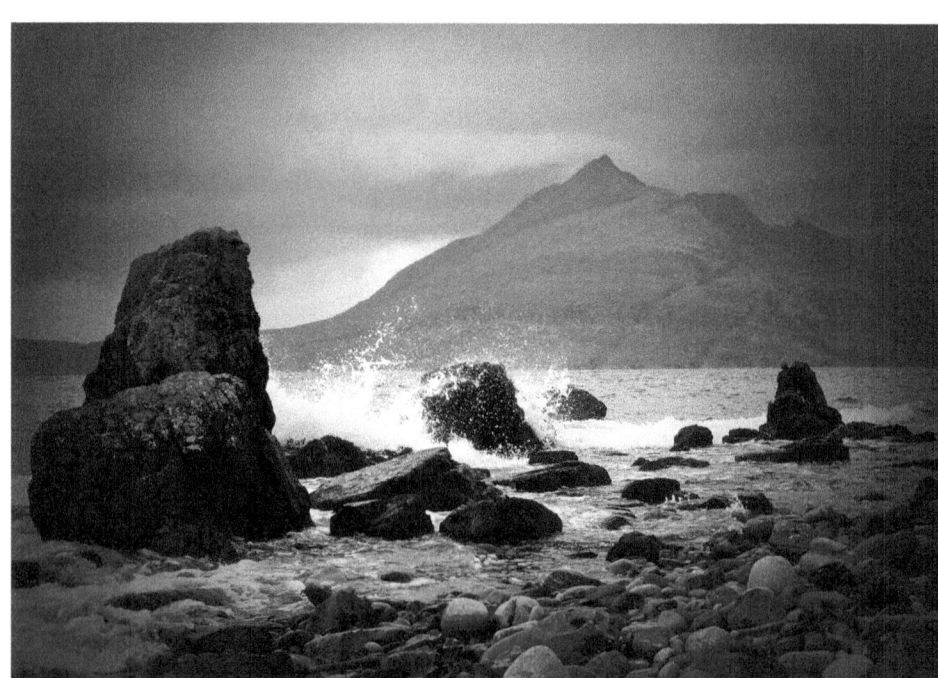

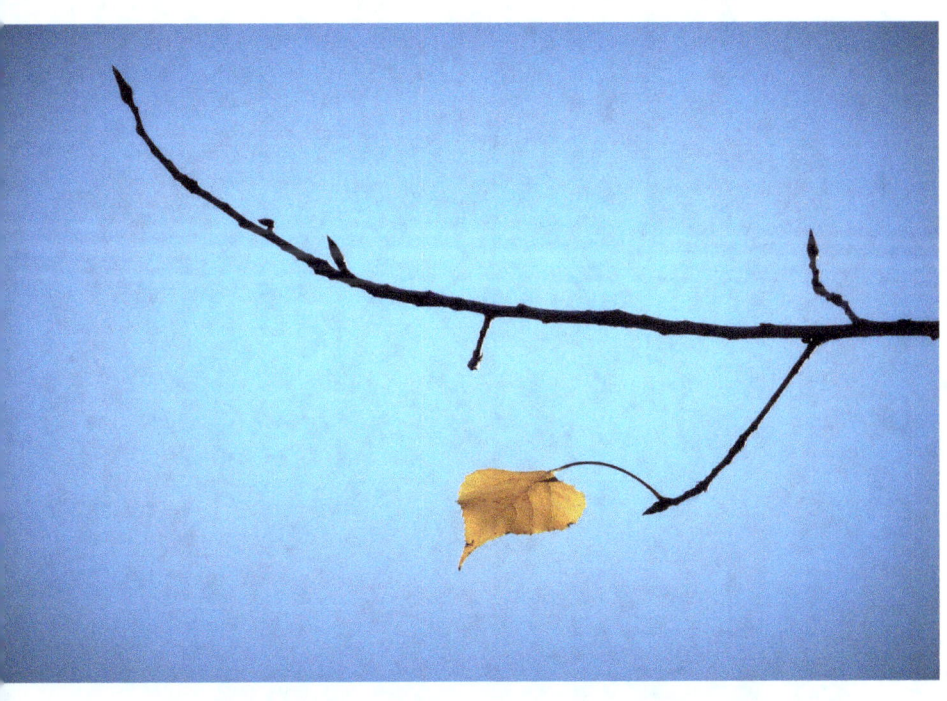

## Psalm 103:2 (NRSV)

"Bless the Lord, O my soul,
and do not forget all his benefits."

Some of his benefits are
Little Things
no bigger than a sparrow—

a piece of grass moving in the breeze
a caterpillar crawling across my path
dandelion puffs standing quietly
a pine cone sitting in the shade
a blossom petal wilting on the path
an ordinary rock resting by the stream
autumn's last golden leaf holding on to its branch
a wasp searching for something on a twig
rose hips glowing on a thorny bush

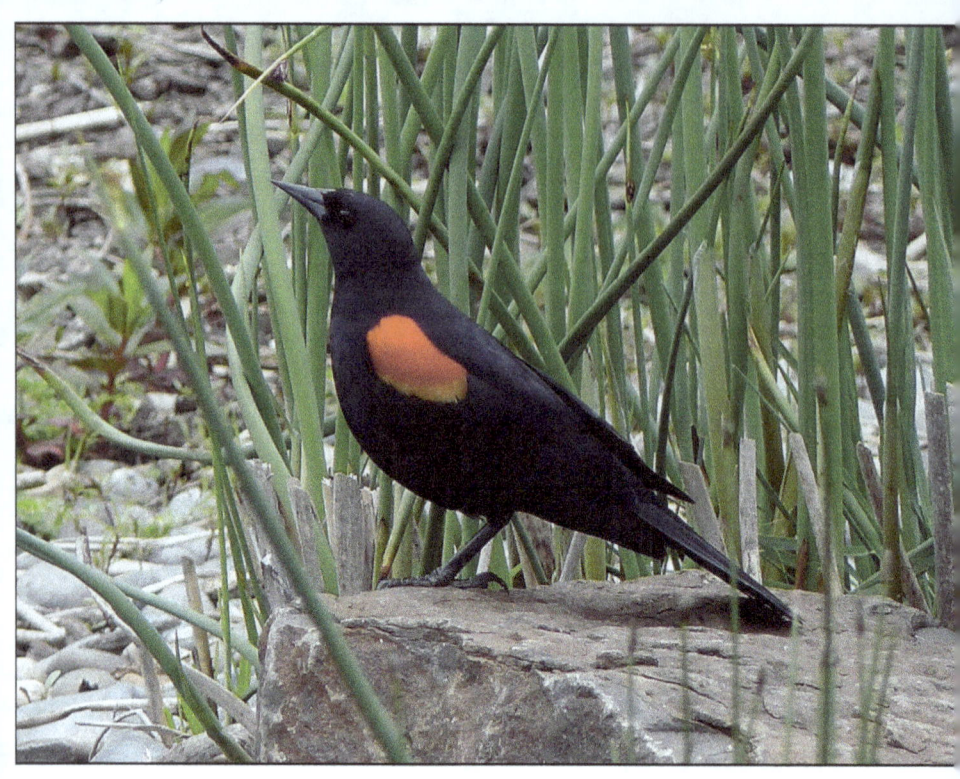

Psalm 25:1 (NKJV)

"To You, O Lord, I lift up my soul."

I hear a great tumult in the cattails.
A crowd of blackbirds is singing
and shouting.
Suddenly they stop
and whoosh up to the sky—
taking me with them.
They circle around
and suddenly drop down
bringing me to earth again
as the commotion begins anew.

## JOHN 14:27 (CEV)

"I give you peace,
the kind of peace that only I can give."

When I watch birds
I'm free as swallows flying in the clouds.
When I feel a breeze
I'm free as wind wandering over the hills.
When I walk in rain
I'm free as raindrops falling on the grass.
When I stroll through wildflowers
I'm free as bluebells dancing in the sun.

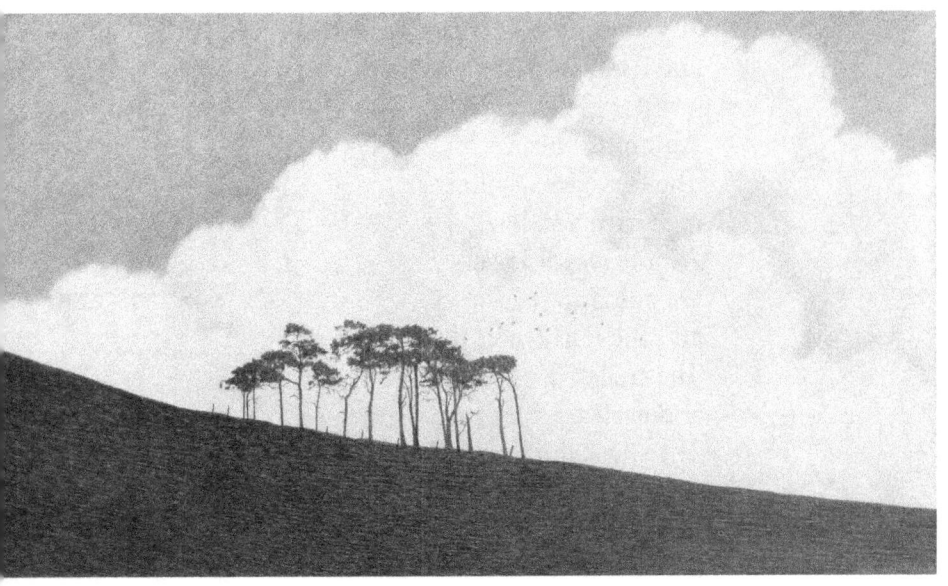

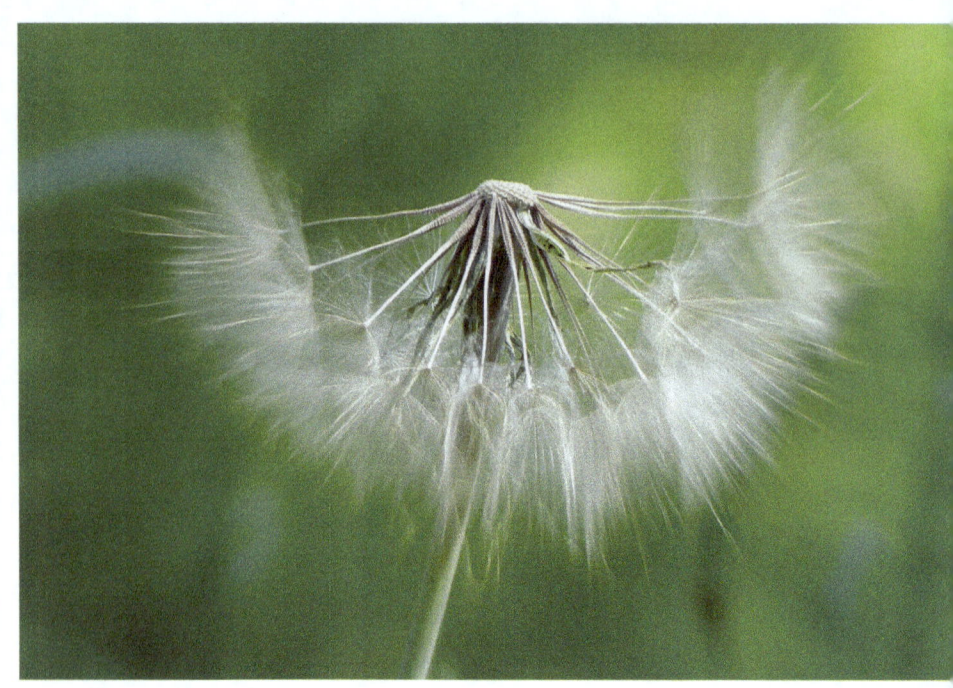

## ECCLESIASTES 3:1 (CEV)

"Everything on earth has its own time
and its own season."

Autumn is near.
The last days of summer
are warm and hazy.
All the weed flowers
are going to seed
and the fluffy ones float in the air.
The creek isn't saying much now
and even the birds are silent.
The sky is dull and tired
with no clouds to enhance its blue.
Dry leaves lie motionless on my path
and distant mountains rest
in soft haze.

PSALM 147:8 (NIV)

He covers the sky with clouds;
he supplies the earth with rain
and makes grass grow on the hills."

The day is wet
though it isn't raining.
Puddles on the path
reflect the trees above
and the damp leaves
have been walked on.

Rows of shining drip circles
hang from bare branches
and deer tracks
wander through the mud
beside the path.
Fresh wind
has cooled the air
and dark clouds hover
over heavy fog.

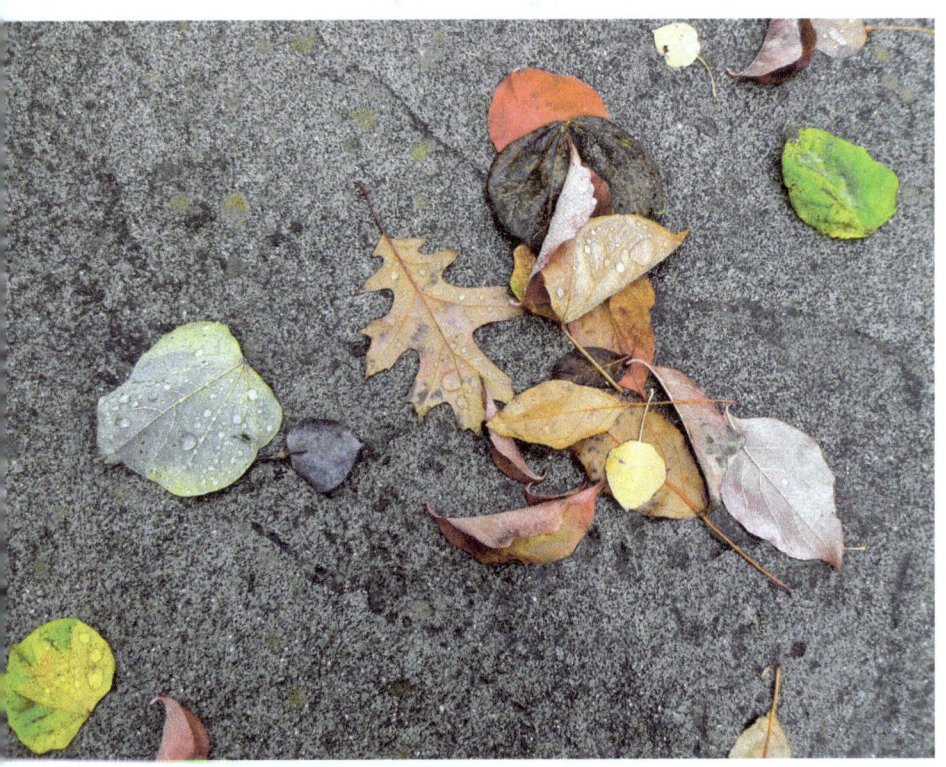

41

## II Thessalonians 3:16 (NCV)

"Now may the Lord of peace
give you peace at all times and in every way."

In my dream I have the whole day
to sit by the shore
with arctic terns flying over
or to walk along the lava-stone beach
with oystercatchers and sandpipers.
Or maybe I'll just sit on the grass
and read a book for a while
taking time to rest in warm sunshine
and fresh sea air.
Perhaps I'll see a seal dozing by the water
with whooper swans floating by.
I know I'll see little eiders with their mothers
and probably greylag geese too.
The day will go by too quickly
because there is so much to see
and think about.

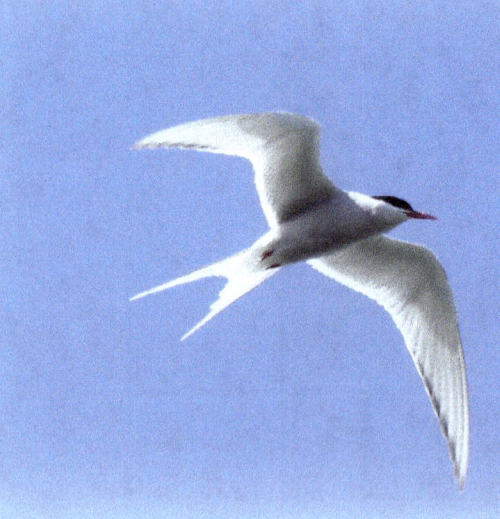

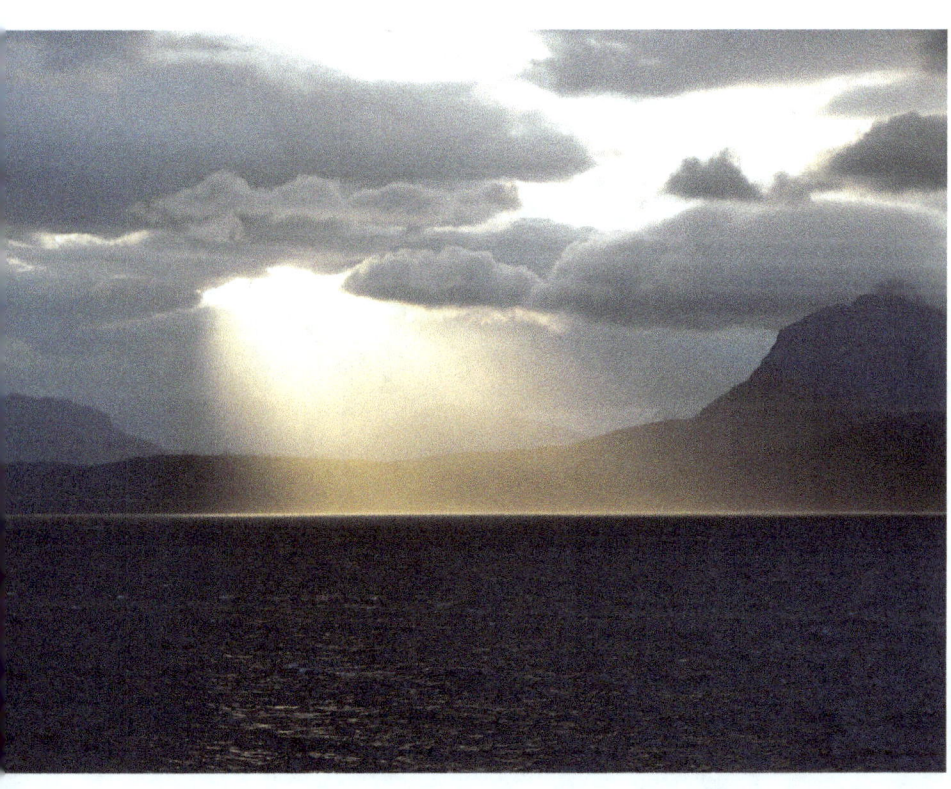

PSALM 19:1 (TEV)

"How clearly the sky reveals God's glory!
How plainly it shows what he has done!"

Brilliant sunsets reveal his glory
along with bright white thunderclouds
or dark black storm fronts.
Lightning flashing across the sky
and the sun warming the earth on a winter morning
show what he has done.
He is revealed in the moon reflected on a quiet lake
and in stars glowing in the dark night.
What he has done is shown in a rainbow
shining across the evening sky,
in snow, and in the cold beauty of aurora borealis.
Yes, the sky clearly shows God's glory.

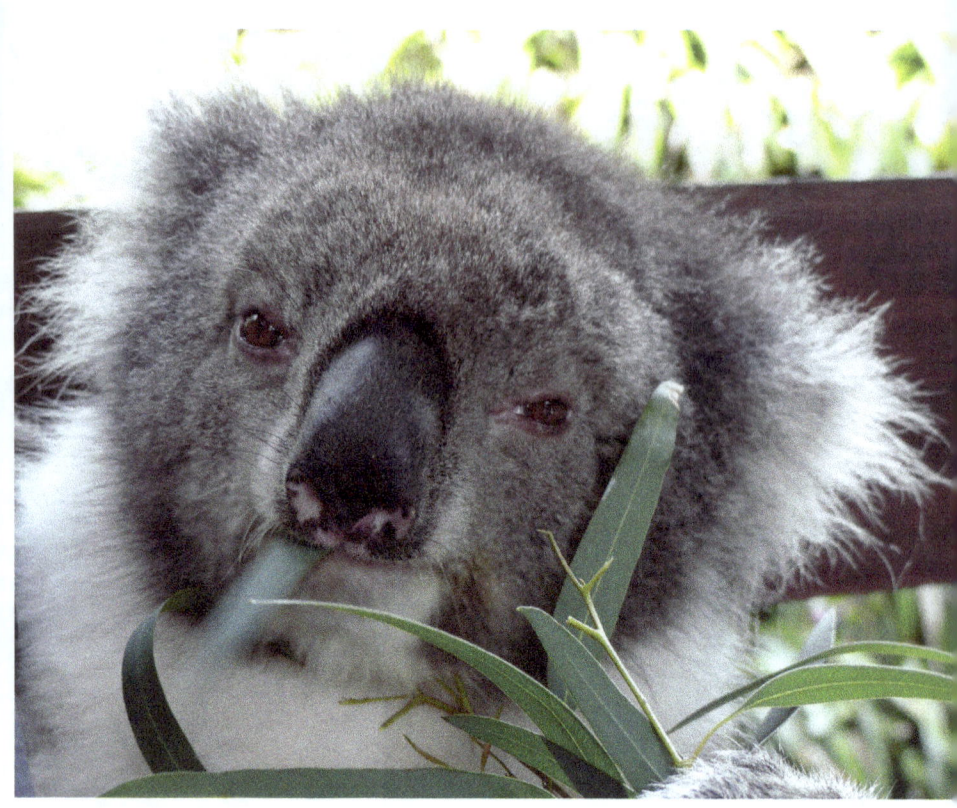

PSALM 9:1, 2 (NRSV)

"I will give thanks to the Lord with my whole heart"—
    thanks for the little hopping mouse that looked at me with love
    and kookaburras laughing by the Howqua River.

"I will tell of all your wonderful deeds"—
    creating a soft little koala named Violet for me to hug
    and fairy penguins to watch coming from the ocean at sunset.

"I will be glad and exult in you"
    because I saw four echidnas in the wild
    and listened to warbling magpies in the morning.

"I will sing praise to your name, O Most High,"
    for trips to Australia
    and visits with all my friends there.

## PHILIPPIANS 4:8 (KJV)

"Whatsoever things are true,"
    that's blackbird songs
    and robin chirps;
"whatsoever things are honest,"
    that's baby ducks
    and pine trees;
"whatsoever things are just,"
    that's radiant sunlight
    and shining stars;
"whatsoever things are pure,"
    that's windy clouds
    and bright tulips;

"whatsoever things are lovely,"
    that's sparkling dewdrops
    and tall waving grass;
"whatsoever things are of good report,"
    that's quail chatter
    and aspen whispers;
"if there be any virtue,
    and if there be any praise,
    think on these things."

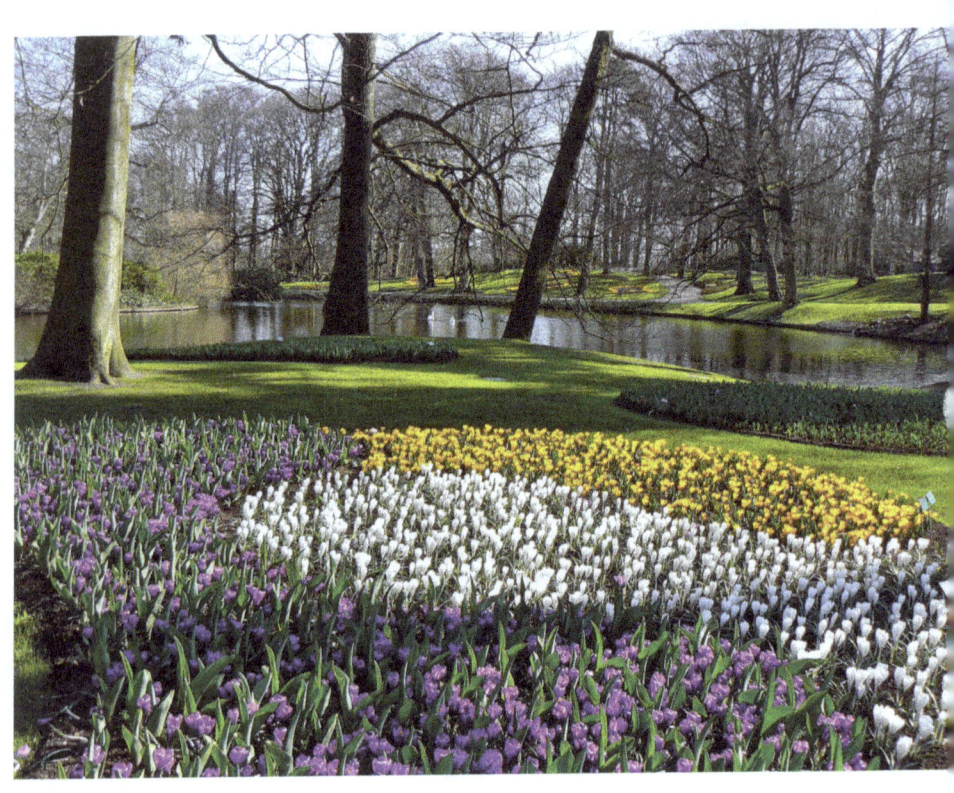

I CORINTHIANS 2:9 (NKJV)

"Eye has not seen, nor ear heard,
nor have entered into the heart of man
the things which God has prepared
for those who love him."

If we have seen Keukenhof in springtime
or Drummond Castle Gardens in autumn
our eyes still have not seen what God has prepared.

If we have heard the dawn chorus early on a May morning
or Doros singing in St. Basil's Cathedral
our ears still have not heard what God has prepared.

Even if we have been lifted by the mist rising up the Quiraing
or felt the stillness of northern Lapland fells
our hearts cannot yet fully know the peace
God has prepared for those who love him.

# Acknowledgments and Notes

Thank you to the people who made this book possible: a friend whose appreciation of my writing gave me the courage to allow it to be seen; Henry Neufeld, a competent and considerate publisher, who thought my art and writing worth publishing and who expertly translated some Scripture specifically for this book; Tom Wehtje, a son-in-law, and another special person who wishes to remain anonymous, who gave valuable writing suggestions; and Paul Johnson, a nephew, who took time to skillfully edit my art photos.

I also appreciate the people who contributed to this book in other ways. The late Roy and Karma Fowler were friends who encouraged me to pursue my interest in art. Jerry Schoepflin, a friend and physician, helped enable me to do it by diagnosing and treating my Lyme disease. Tom Emmerson and the late Ken MacKintosh, my art teachers at Walla Walla College/University, made a great difference in the development of my artistic ability.

Art and photography help me keep special nature experiences alive. I draw directly from nature or use only my own photos for reference for my drawings and paintings because that makes art more meaningful to me, but I rearrange, combine, and stylize at times. Bob Bond, a brother-in-law and excellent photographer, has given me helpful photography advice. Art classes in composition and design also helped improve my photography.

The experience of living in "The Garden Cottage" in a woods at Earlyvale, near Eddleston, Scotland, while my husband worked on doctoral studies at the University of Edinburgh was particularly important in deepening my love of nature. A friend, the late John Ogilvie, contributed much to my knowledge and appreciation of Scottish wildflowers and wildlife.

I also want to express my gratitude for my late parents, Lee and Myra Hoffman, who encouraged my interests in nature, art, and photography.

I am especially grateful to my family. Our daughters and their husbands, Karin Thompson and Tom Wehtje, and Krista and Steve Smith, are a great inspiration to me. Finally, I want to thank my husband, Alden, whose love supports me in all I do and who values my art and writing far more than they deserve. His suggestions for this book were especially helpful and without his encouragement it never would have been published.

"Give thanks to the Lord, for he is good. His love endures forever" Psalm 136:1 (NIV).

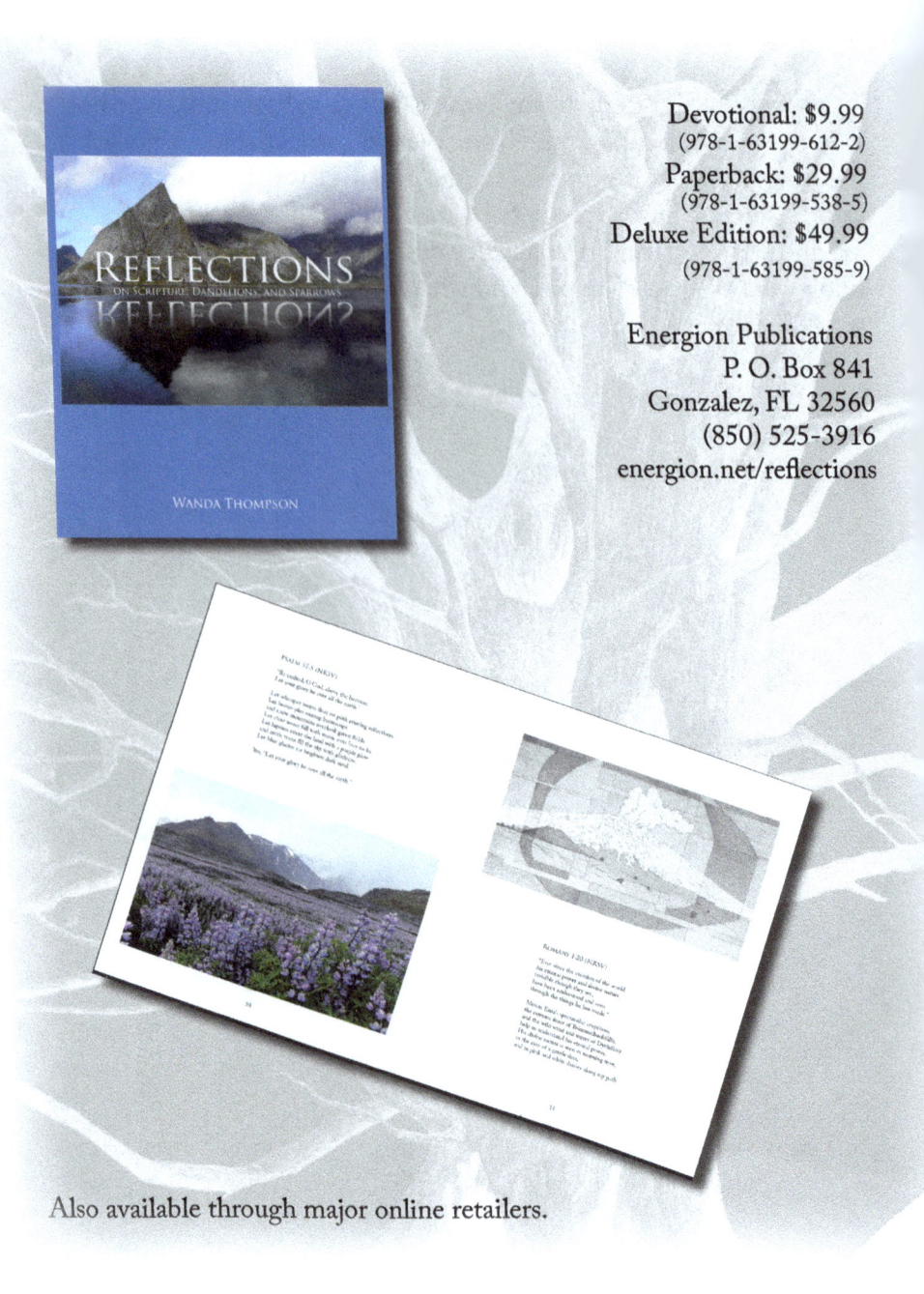

Devotional: $9.99
(978-1-63199-612-2)
Paperback: $29.99
(978-1-63199-538-5)
Deluxe Edition: $49.99
(978-1-63199-585-9)

Energion Publications
P. O. Box 841
Gonzalez, FL 32560
(850) 525-3916
energion.net/reflections

Also available through major online retailers.

www.ingramcontent.com/pod-product-compliance
Lightning Source LLC
Chambersburg PA
CBHW051245170526
45165CB00004B/1585